THE WORLD'S MOST
AMAZING CASTLES

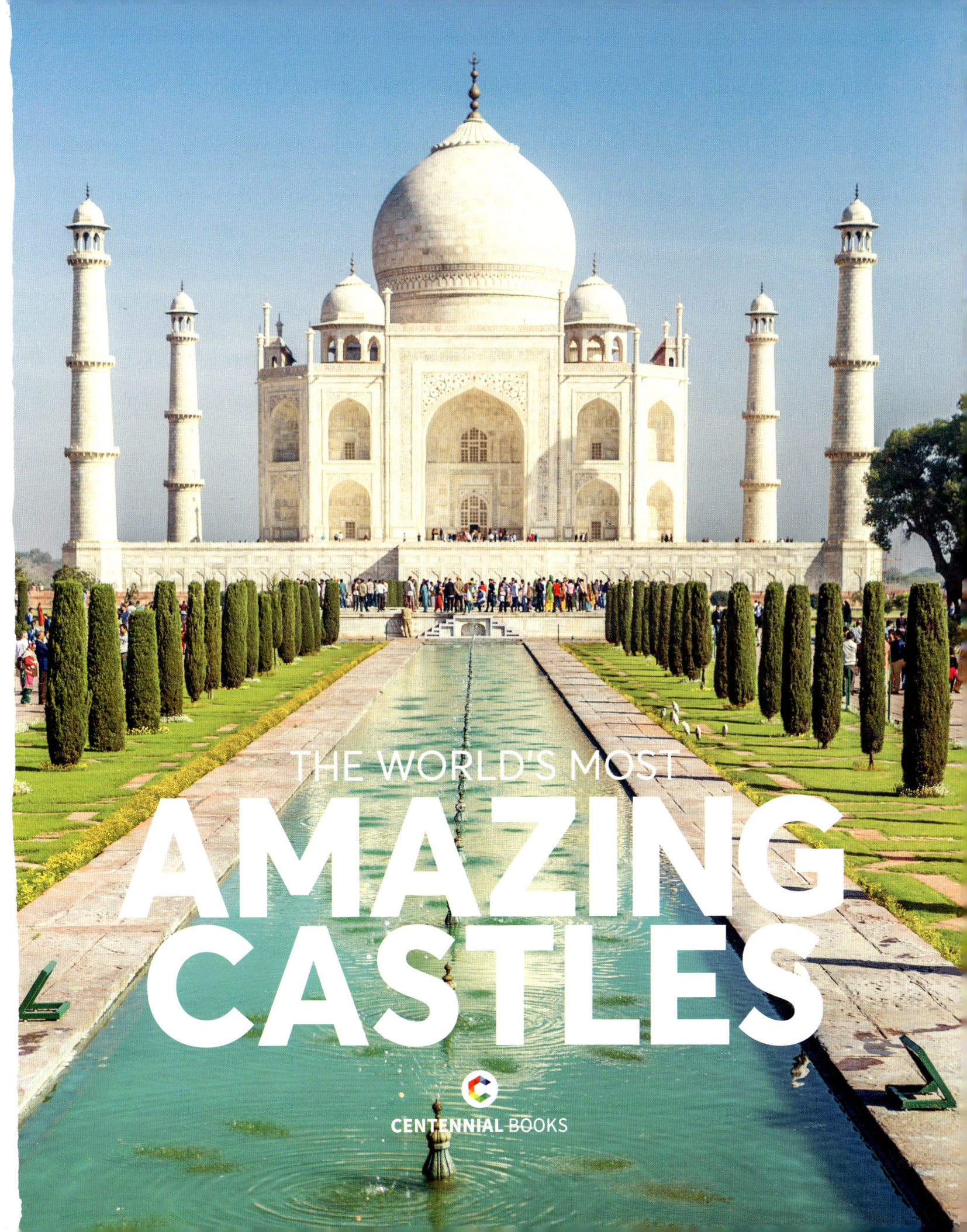

CENTENNIAL BOOKS

Castello de Amorosa, a medieval-inspired Tuscan castle and winery, sits in California's lush Napa Valley.

CENTENNIAL BOOKS

THE WORLD'S MOST
AMAZING CASTLES

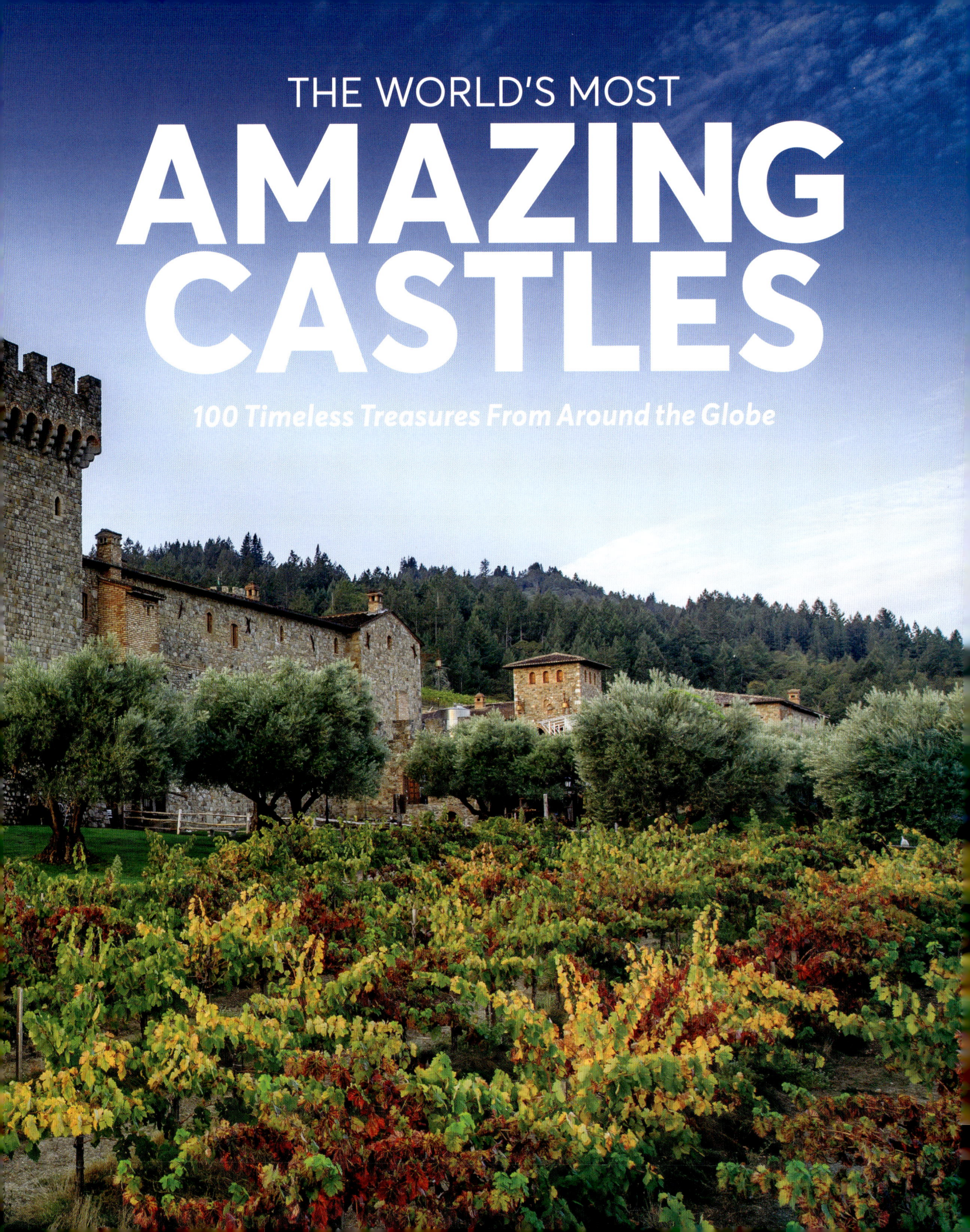

100 Timeless Treasures From Around the Globe

At more than 1,000 years old, the Mont Saint Michel abbey in Normandy, France is one of the grandest buildings in Europe.

4 THE WORLD'S MOST AMAZING CASTLES

CONTENTS

FOREWORD
8 | Living in a Castle
Lady Fiona, 8th Countess of Carnarvon, and owner of Highclere Castle (home of the real-life Downton Abbey), shares what it's like to own one of the most famous homes in the world, and the pleasures and responsibilities that come with living on a magnificent estate.

CHAPTER ONE
12 | British Isles, Ireland & Scandinavia
Kiss the Blarney Stone, gaze at Scotland's crown jewels and roam ornate chambers once trod by kings, queens, knights and nobles at these ancient homes. Plus: A-list castles that have graced the silver screen.

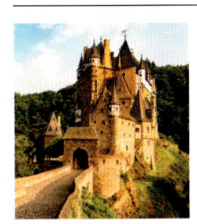

CHAPTER TWO
46 | Germany and Austria
Famous for their lofty perches that pierce the clouds, Germany and Austria's soaring schlosses have inspired composers, poets, novelists, filmmakers and even the likes of Walt Disney. Plus: New world beauties that rival their European counterparts.

CHAPTER THREE
72 | France and Switzerland
These châteaux are arguably the most beautiful in the world. And colorful characters, from Joan of Arc to Marie Antoinette, bring their rich histories to life. Plus: Short-term rentals where you can feel like king or queen for at least a little while.

CHAPTER FOUR
102 | Southern Europe
From Portugal's eccentric palaces and Spain's Moorish fortresses to Italy's seaside citadels, the castles of southern Europe blend majestic architecture with a balmy Mediterranean climate. Plus: Fine wineries where historic intrigue meets robust reds and whites.

CHAPTER FIVE
130 | Eastern Europe
Russian empresses, Transylvanian counts, Bohemian kings and Prussian knights haunt the halls of the castles dotting Romania, Poland, the Czech Republic and beyond. Plus: Royal hotels where history and spectacular settings combine for a memorable stay.

CHAPTER SIX
158 | Asia and Middle East
Samurai strongholds, a forbidden fortress, the world's most famous monument to love—they're all in these ancient locales, where the castles of Japan, China, India and more defy classification. Plus: Grandeur and reverence come together at these sublime monasteries and convents.

ON THE COVER Neuschwanstein Castle, located in southern Germany, is the stuff of fairy tales (it even inspired Disney's Cinderella castle) and is spectacular in any season.

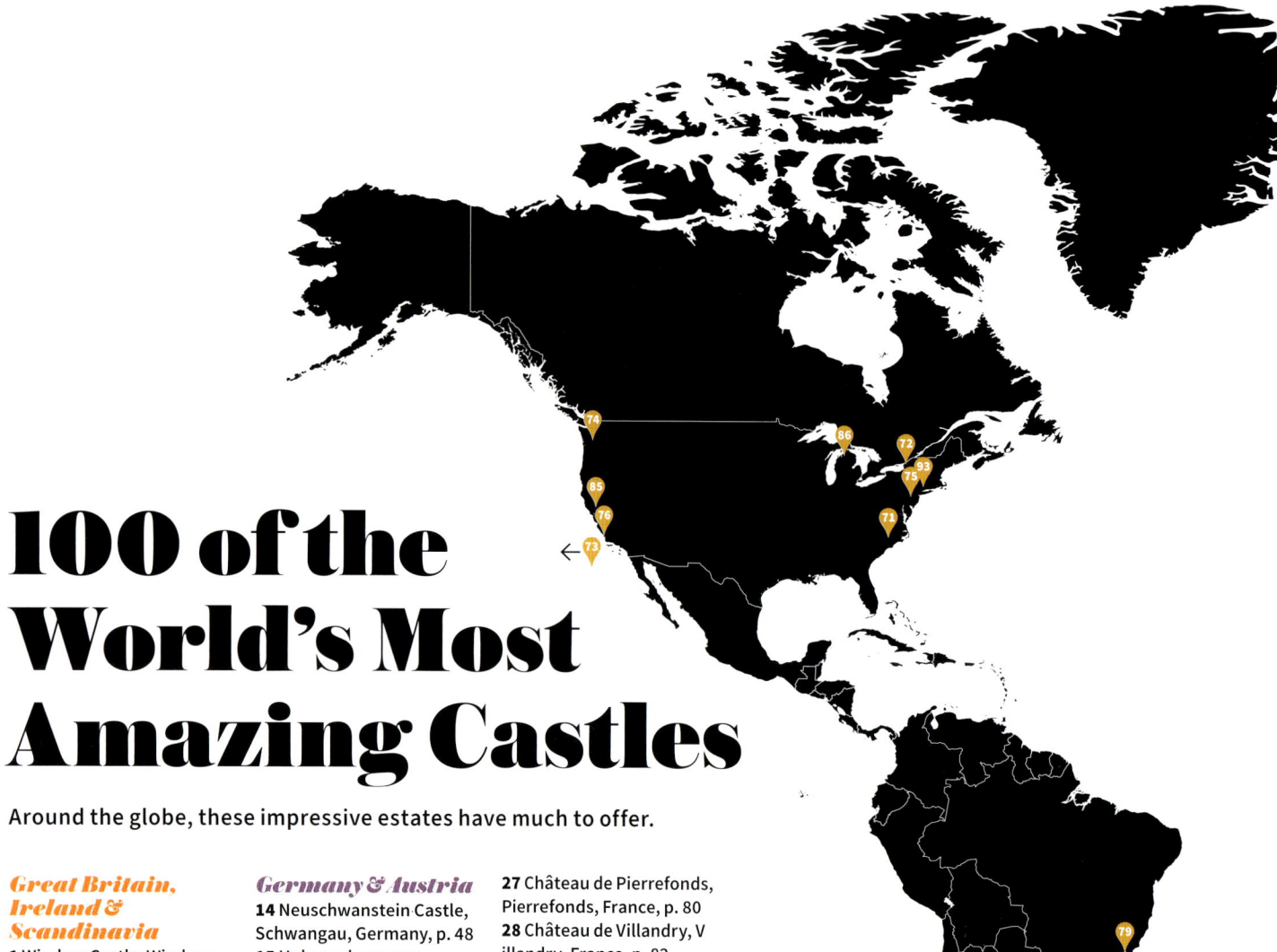

100 of the World's Most Amazing Castles

Around the globe, these impressive estates have much to offer.

Great Britain, Ireland & Scandinavia
1 Windsor Castle, Windsor, England, p. 14
2 Leeds Castle, Maidstone, Kent, England, p. 18
3 Bodiam Castle, Robertsbridge, East Sussex, England, p. 20
4 Highclere Castle, Hampshire, England, p. 22
5 Conwy Castle, Conwy, Wales, p. 24
6 Edinburgh Castle, Edinburgh, Scotland, p. 26
7 Dunnottar Castle, Stonehaven, Scotland, p. 28
8 Kilkenny Castle, Collegepark, County Kilkenny, Ireland, p. 30
9 Blarney Castle, Monacnapa, Blarney, County Cork, Ireland, p. 32
10 Dromoland Castle, County Clare, Ireland, p. 34
11 Kronborg Castle, Helsingør, Denmark, p. 36
12 Egeskov Castle, Isle of Funen, Denmark, p. 38
13 Örebro Castle, Örebro, Sweden, p. 40

Germany & Austria
14 Neuschwanstein Castle, Schwangau, Germany, p. 48
15 Hohenschwangau Castle, Hohenschwangau, Germany p. 51
16 Lichtenstein Castle, Lichtenstein, Germany, p. 52
17 Heidelberg Castle, Heidelberg, Germany, p. 54
18 Schwerin Castle, Schwerin, Germany, p. 56
19 Eltz Castle, Wierschem, Germany, p. 58
20 Hohenzollern Castle, Bisingen, Germany, p. 60
21 Artstetten Castle, Artstetten-Pöbring, Austria, p. 62
22 Hohenwerfen Castle, Werfen, Austria, p. 64
23 Hohensalzburg Castle, Salzburg, Austria, p. 66

France & Switzerland
24 Château de Chenonceau, Chenonceaux, France, p. 74
25 Château de Chambord, Chambord, France, p. 76
26 Château du Haut-Koenigsbourg, Orschwiller, France, p. 78
27 Château de Pierrefonds, Pierrefonds, France, p. 80
28 Château de Villandry, Villandry, France, p. 82
29 Château de Sully-sur-Loire, Sully-sur-Loire, France, p. 84
30 Palace of Versailles, Versailles, France, p. 86
31 Château de Chaumont-sur-Loire, Chaumont-sur-Loire, France, p. 90
32 Gruyères Castle, Gruyères, Fribourg, Switzerland, p. 92
33 Chillon Castle, Veytaux, Vaud, Switzerland, p. 94
34 Oberhofen Castle, Oberhofen, Switzerland, p. 96

Southern Europe
35 Alcazar of Segovia, Segovia, Spain, p. 104
36 Castillo de Coca, Coca, Spain, p. 106
37 Alhambra, Granada, Spain, p. 108
38 Pena Palace, Sintra, Portugal, p. 112
39 Aragonese Castle, Ischia, Italy, p. 114
40 Miramare Castle, Trieste, Italy, p. 116
41 Rocca Scaligera, Sirmione, Italy, p. 118
42 Guaita Castle, City of San Marino, Republic of San Marino, p. 120
43 Kyrenia Castle, Kyrenia, Cyprus, p. 122
44 Palace of the Grand Master of the Knights, Rhodes, Greece, p. 124

Eastern Europe
45 Bran Castle, Bran, Romania, p. 132
46 Malbork Castle, Malbork, Poland, p. 134
47 Prague Castle, Prague, Czech Republic, p. 136
48 Hluboká Castle, Hluboká Nad Vltavou, Czech Republic, p. 138
49 Karlštejn Castle, Karlštejn, Czech Republic, p. 140
50 Catherine Palace, Pushkin, Russia, p. 142
51 Garibaldi Castle, Khryashchevka, p. 146
52 Swallow's Nest, Yalta, Crimea, p. 148
53 Trakošćan Castle, Bednja, Croatia, p. 150
54 Kamerlengo Castle, Trogir, Croatia, p. 152

6 THE WORLD'S MOST AMAZING CASTLES

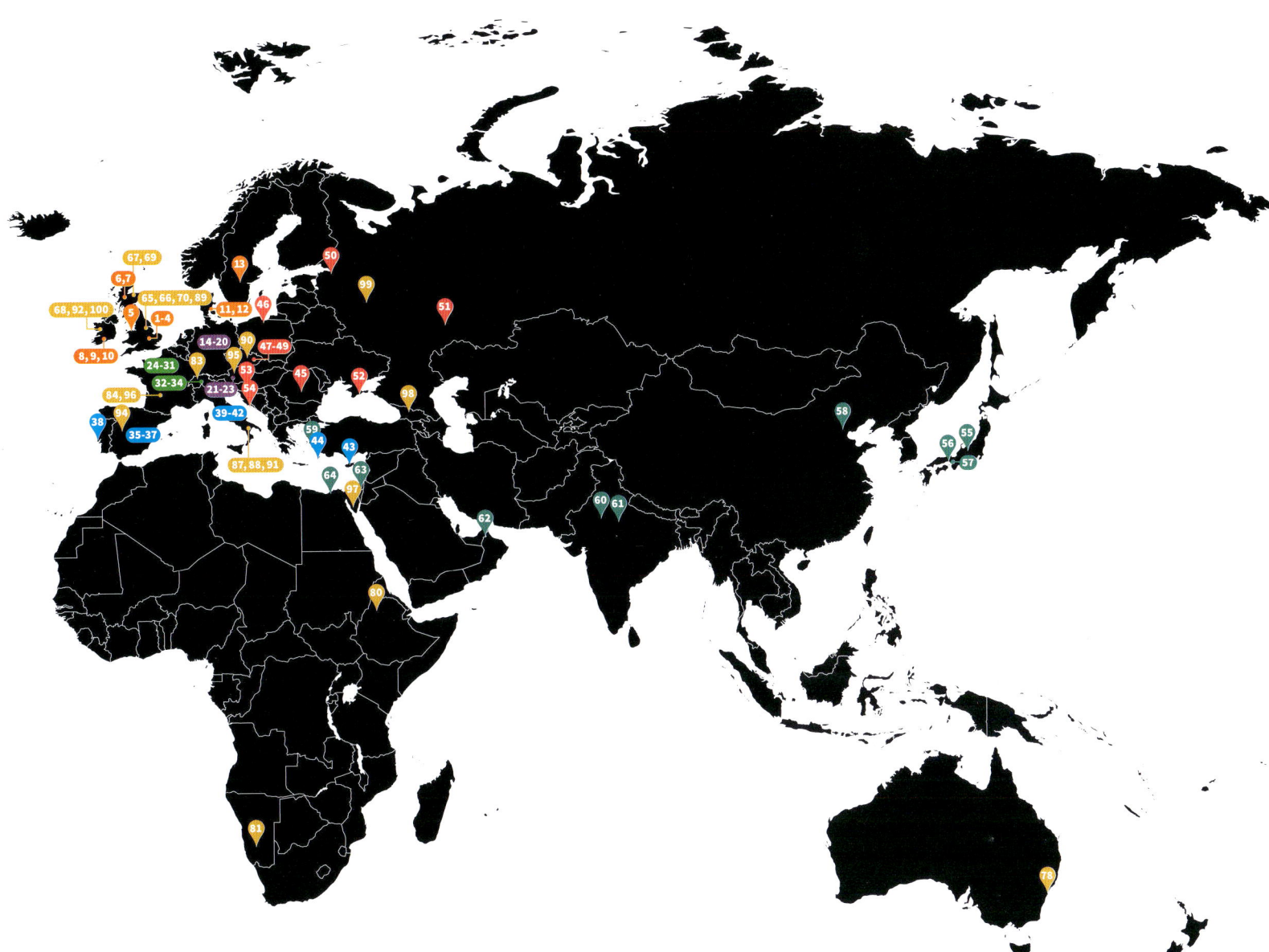

Asia & the Middle East

55 Matsumoto Castle, Matsumoto, Japan, p. 160
56 Himeji Castle, Himeji, Japan, p. 162
57 Osaka Castle, Osaka, Japan, p. 164
58 Forbidden City, Beijing, China, p. 166
59 Bodrum Castle, Bodrum, Turkey, p. 168
60 Amber Fort, Jaipur, India, p. 170
61 Taj Mahal, Agra, India, p. 172
62 Al Jahili Fort, Al Ain, United Arab Emirates, p. 176
63 Tower of David, Jerusalem, Israel, p. 178
64 Citadel of Qaitbay, Alexandria, Egypt, p. 180

More to Explore

65 Alnwick Castle, Alnwick, England, p. 42
66 Bamburgh Castle, Bamburgh, England, p. 44
67 Doune Castle, Doune, Scotland, p. 44
68 Trim Castle, Trim, County Meath, Ireland, p. 44
69 Eileen Donan Castle, Kyle of Lochalsh, Scotland, p. 45
70 Castle Howard, York, England, p. 45
71 Biltmore Estate, Asheville, North Carolina, p. 68
72 Boldt Castle, Alexandria, New York, p. 70
73 Iolani Palace, Honolulu, Hawaii, p. 70
74 Thornewood Castle, Lakewood, Washington, p. 71
75 Fonthill Castle, Doylestown, Pennsylvania, p. 71
76 Hearst Castle, San Simeon, California, p. 71
77 Wulff Castle, Viña del Mar, Chile, p. 98
78 Government House, Sydney, Australia, p. 100
79 Ilha Fiscal, Guanabara Bay, Brazil, p. 100
80 Fasil Ghebbi, Ethiopia, p. 100
81 Duwisib Castle, Southern Namib Region, Namibia, p. 101
82 Palacio de Aguas Corrientes, Buenos Aires, Argentina, p. 101
83 Aigle Castle, Aigle, Switzerland, p. 126
84 Château de Pitray, Gardegan-et-Tourtirac, France, p. 128
85 Castello di Amorosa, Calistoga, California, p. 128
86 Castle Farms, Charlevoix, Michigan, p. 129
87 Castello di Oliveto, Castelfiorentino, Italy, p. 129
88 Castello di Brolio, Gaiole in Chianti, Italy, p. 129
89 Warwick Castle, Warwick, England, p. 154
90 Chateau Herálec Boutique Hotel & Spa by L'Occitane, Herálec, Czech Republic, p. 156
91 Castello di Pavone, Pavone Canavese, Italy, p. 156
92 Ashford Castle, Cong, Ireland, p. 156
93 Castle Hotel & Spa, Tarrytown, New York, p. 157
94 Parador Oropesa, Oropesa, Spain, p. 157
95 Melk Abbey, Melk, Austria, p. 182
96 Mount-Saint-Michel, Normandy, France, p. 183
97 Saint Catherine's Monastery, South Sinai Governorate, Egypt, p. 183
98 Gergeti Trinity Chirch, Kazbegi, Oni, Georgia, p. 185
99 Novodevichy Convent, Moscow, Russia, p. 185
100 Kylemore Abbey, Connemara, County Galway, Ireland, p. 184

FOREWORD

Living in a Castle

Lady Fiona, the Countess of Carnarvon, shares what it's like to reside in one of the world's most famous homes— Highclere Castle, the main filming location for *Downton Abbey*.

MANY OF OUR MYTHS AND LEGENDS BEGIN WITH castles. They may be enormous fortified buildings with turrets and towers to offer protection and give advance views of potential marauders, or they may incorporate sumptuous works of art and interiors to indicate wealth and prestige. Alternatively, a "castle" might be built just as a beautiful architectural achievement, a celebration of love.

Castles are part of our dreams and our imaginations, encompassing both secret fears of the deepest of dungeons and the tangible expression of success, power and wealth in soaring turrets and spires. Most people will not live in a castle, yet we can all dream of fairy-tale princes and princesses. We can contemplate all that the word "castle" represents and in our reveries build them in our minds with no rules of architecture or finance.

The 100 castles in this book are all extraordinarily impressive, built by the richest and most ambitious families, to reflect the rules and achievements of their time: the perspectives, politics and styles of their owners. They have foundations, histories and have, over the centuries, served many purposes.

I spent my childhood in Cornwall, England, near Tintagel Castle, impossibly romantic with sea mists and tales of knights, magical swords, jousts and beautiful ladies. I am not sure how much truth is in these tales, but the ruins give them authenticity and converts the stories into history. I have loved, and still love, those legends, and am drawn every time to visit and walk the ramparts, imaging those who might have lived there 1,000 years ago.

Today, of course, I do live in a castle and one which has perhaps become one of the most famous homes in the world through its alter ego, "Downton Abbey." If the world assumes that Highclere was built as a celebration of Victorian times, that is just the latest story. There has been a home and a building on this site since 749 A.D., when the foundations of the late Saxon house are recorded in no fewer than five Anglo-Saxon charters from that date when the buildings and estate were given to the Bishops of Winchester.

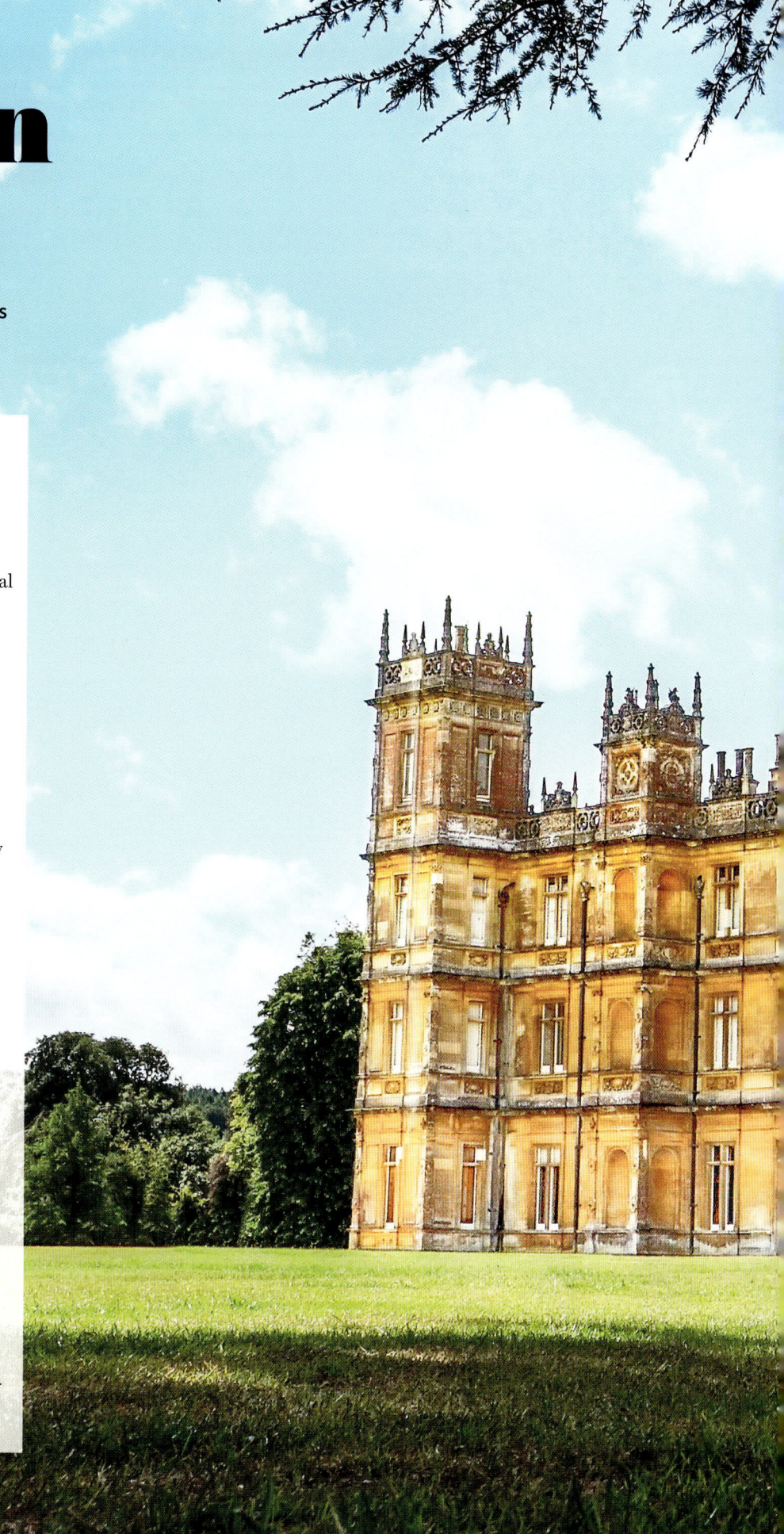

Thousands of people come each year to visit Highclere, the real-life Downton Abbey.

Bishop William of Wykeham built a medieval palace and gardens on the park back in the 14th century.

FOREWORD

The south-facing Music Room features 16th-century Italian tapestries. Today, the Eighth Earl and Countess of Carnarvon (inset) still live on the estate.

By the 14th century, Highclere had been transformed into a palace, with treasured books, walled gardens, fish ponds, rabbit warrens and a deer park. At this time, Bishop William of Wykeham lived here whilst he was building Windsor Castle for King Edward III. Overall, it was owned by the Bishops of Winchester for some 800 years, and it has more or less stood on the same footprint as that on which it stands today; the old medieval walls lie within the walls of the current castle.

From a palace, it became an elegant Tudor family residence, which is the home my husband's ancestor bought in 1679. Later, the Carnarvon family built a symmetrical classical stone Georgian home around the Elizabethan building, which stood until the Third Earl of Carnarvon commissioned the preeminent Victorian architect Sir Charles Barry to design and build the castle known and loved today. Barry was inspired by his travels in Italy, by the colors and sights he saw there; he regarded Highclere as perhaps his most successful project, and one that was far more enjoyable than his contemporaneous one: The Houses of Parliament.

Initially, Highclere was called a palace (once again) before being renamed Highclere Castle. It has a cozy splendor with between 250 and 300 rooms, and sits in 1,000 acres of Capability Brown parkland. We still look after farmland, downland and woodland of another 4,500 acres.

It sits in the middle of its own arcadia: It is a castle and very real, but also a dream. Yet the highlights for me lie beyond the castle building. It is the setting, the sense of place, the deep knowledge of history which plumbs us into the ground, the generations of us who lived, strove and laughed here before my husband and myself. It is an anchor and a reassurance, a visible reminder of our achievements and heritage.

If an Englishman's home is his castle, few people live and look after the genuine article. It is a privilege, a responsibility and an extraordinarily busy life at all hours alongside a community who love this building and all it stands for. It does sometimes feel as if I am just "multi-muddling" along whilst pretending to be a swan.

Highclere's heritage touches some of the castles explored in this book, from Windsor Castle and Bishop William of Wykeham, to a beautiful treasured Agra carpet from the home city of the Taj Mahal. The Fifth Countess of Carnarvon gifted some important French furniture to Versailles Palace, and one of Highclere's most important desks is that of Napoleon I by Jacobs Frères, which sits in pride of place in a gilded salon.

Bran Castle and Edinburgh Castle are very different from Highclere: two fortified castles with far darker stories to share. Pena Palace in Portugal has a more reflective and diplomatic history, whilst Miramare Castle was built in the late 19th century and, although much altered, survived the ravages of two world wars. The Alhambra is both a palace and a fortress, uniting architecture, religion and culture in one extraordinary World Heritage Site. Leeds Castle was home to several queens of England, whilst Neuschwanstein Castle seems the ultimate Disney fantasy where anything is possible

But like Highclere, they are more than just castles. They stand for values, cultures and dreams. As Victor Hugo said: "If you don't build castles in the air, you won't build anything on the ground."

— *LADY FIONA, EIGHTH COUNTESS OF CARNARVON*

Dutch paintings from the 17th century hang in the Smoking Room; they are some of the earliest works of art brought to Highclere by the Carnarvon family.

CHAPTER 1

Great Britain, IRELAND & Scandinavia

KISS THE BLARNEY STONE, GAZE AT SCOTLAND'S CROWN JEWELS AND ROAM ORNATE CHAMBERS ONCE TROD BY KINGS, QUEENS, KNIGHTS AND NOBLES AT THESE ANCIENT HOMES.

Now in ruins, Dunnottar, located in Stonehaven, Scotland, was once considered one of the strongest castles in the country.

GREAT BRITAIN, IRELAND & SCANDINAVIA

ARGUABLY THE MOST FAMOUS CASTLE IN the world, Windsor Castle checks all the boxes: crenellated towers, imposing masonry, lavish royal rooms. But this 13-acre estate, which overlooks the River Thames 25 miles west of London, didn't start out as the majestic stone structure it is today. Its nearly 1,000-year history goes back to around 1070, when William the Conqueror began constructing a wooden fortress on the site.

Over the centuries, some 39 kings and queens made their mark on the structure, expanding and redecorating it. Henry I, who married at Windsor Castle in 1121, was the first monarch to use the stronghold as a residence. His grandson Henry II added true royal apartments and began replacing the timber walls with stone. In the 14th century, Edward III restored the castle in Gothic style. But George IV is most credited for giving the palace its current look—fashioning the romantic "castle" facade and extravagantly furnishing the inside in the 1820s.

In 1845, Queen Victoria first opened the State Apartments to the public, and today's visitors can still tour these sumptuous suites, along with the ornate Semi-State Rooms, the gilded Grand Reception Room and the historic St George's Chapel, which hosted the 2018 wedding of Prince Harry and Meghan Markle. Today, the castle continues to be used as a functioning home and a grand venue for state and ceremonial engagements. It is living history in action—a fascinating window into the life of the crown.

Windsor Castle
WINDSOR, ENGLAND

Over the past 900 years, more than 30 monarchs have called Windsor Castle their home.

GREAT BRITAIN, IRELAND & SCANDINAVIA

Queen Elizabeth II passes the majority of her private weekends at Windsor Castle, the biggest and oldest occupied castle on Earth.

16 THE WORLD'S MOST AMAZING CASTLES

Check closure dates in advance at rct.uk before you go and purchase tickets. Alternatively, the **London Pass** grants free entry to Windsor Castle and more than 80 other attractions, including **Westminster Abbey**, the **Tower of London** and others. Don't miss the **Changing of the Guard**; the schedule can be found on the website. On Sundays, the chapel is closed to the public, though visitors are welcome to attend services. Stay at **Coworth Park**, a nearby estate turned hotel that dates to 1776.

The Waterloo Chamber — named in celebration of Napoleon's defeat—is one of the most visited places in the castle.

GREAT BRITAIN, IRELAND & SCANDINAVIA

Leeds Castle

MAIDSTONE, KENT, ENGLAND

ONCE CALLED "THE LOVELIEST CASTLE in the world" by Lord Conway, Leeds Castle is as compelling as it is beautiful. Its tale begins with Robert de Crevecoeur—an Anglo-Norman nobleman who first built a stone fortification on the site in 1119—and culminates with Lady Baillie, an affluent Anglo-American who bought the 500-acre estate in the 1920s.

Over its long history, many other significant players shaped and reshaped the narrative. Its 300-year chapter as a royal residence began in 1278, when it was acquired by Queen Eleanor of Castile, the first wife of King Edward I. Over the years, it became the personal property of six of England's queens, including Catherine of Aragon, whose king, Henry VIII, reworked the formidable stronghold into a lush Tudor palace.

After changing hands several times over the centuries, it was rebuilt in its current Tudor style in 1823. A century later, Lady Baillie became the final private holder to make her mark, swathing the interiors with glamorous furnishings and entertaining the luminaries of the day.

Lady Baillie left the estate to the public, and today more than 600,000 annual visitors enjoy the extravagant rooms, English gardens, maze and playgrounds. In 2019, the castle officially turned 900 years old. As its curators look to the future, Leeds Castle's story is still very much in the making.

Leeds Castle occupies islands in a lake formed by the River Len.

The castle includes a collection of more than 130 dog collars from five different centuries.

Leeds Castle offers a variety of on-site lodging options, including cottages, 1930s Stable Courtyard rooms, 16th-century Maiden's Tower rooms and medieval-style "glamping" tents; entrance fees and a falconry experience are covered in the room rate. Alternately, redeem your Marriott Rewards points at the nearby **Tudor Park Marriott Hotel & Country Club**. Make a reservation at the 17th-century **Castle View Restaurant**; you can't go wrong with fish and chips. For even more medieval discovery, visit **Hever Castle**, 40 miles away.

GREAT BRITAIN, IRELAND & SCANDINAVIA

Bodiam Castle

ROBERTSBRIDGE, EAST SUSSEX, ENGLAND

ITS STRIKING SYMMETRY reflecting evocatively in a wide storybook moat, Bodiam Castle is the stuff of fairy tales. And, in fact, while the castle certainly has defensive features, it was primarily designed to impress.

Built in 1385 by Sir Edward Dalyngrigge, a knight of King Edward III, the grand private residence would have been well-appointed for its time, boasting comfortable household apartments, a great hall for entertaining, landscaped medieval gardens, dozens of fireplaces and almost 30 toilets. Very little of this relative extravagance remains today, as the manor's interior fell to ruin in the 17th century.

Happily, a succession of owners—John Fuller, George Cubitt and Lord Curzon—worked to restore the exterior to its current state, and the property was gifted to the National Trust in 1925. Modern visitors who roam its echoing chambers and spiral staircases can easily imagine what life here might have been like. And indeed, as they gaze out from the top of the battlements to the surrounding Rother Valley, they enjoy a view that has changed little in 600 years.

Remarkably, Bodiam Castle also retains its original wooden portcullis (grated sliding door)—likely the oldest such door in the country. Set dramatically in the center of the twin-towered gatehouse entrance, this relic from distant times is a poignant reminder that while the Middle Ages have long since passed, the spirit of Camelot is alive and well in jolly old England.

Bodiam Castle presides over the East Sussex countryside.

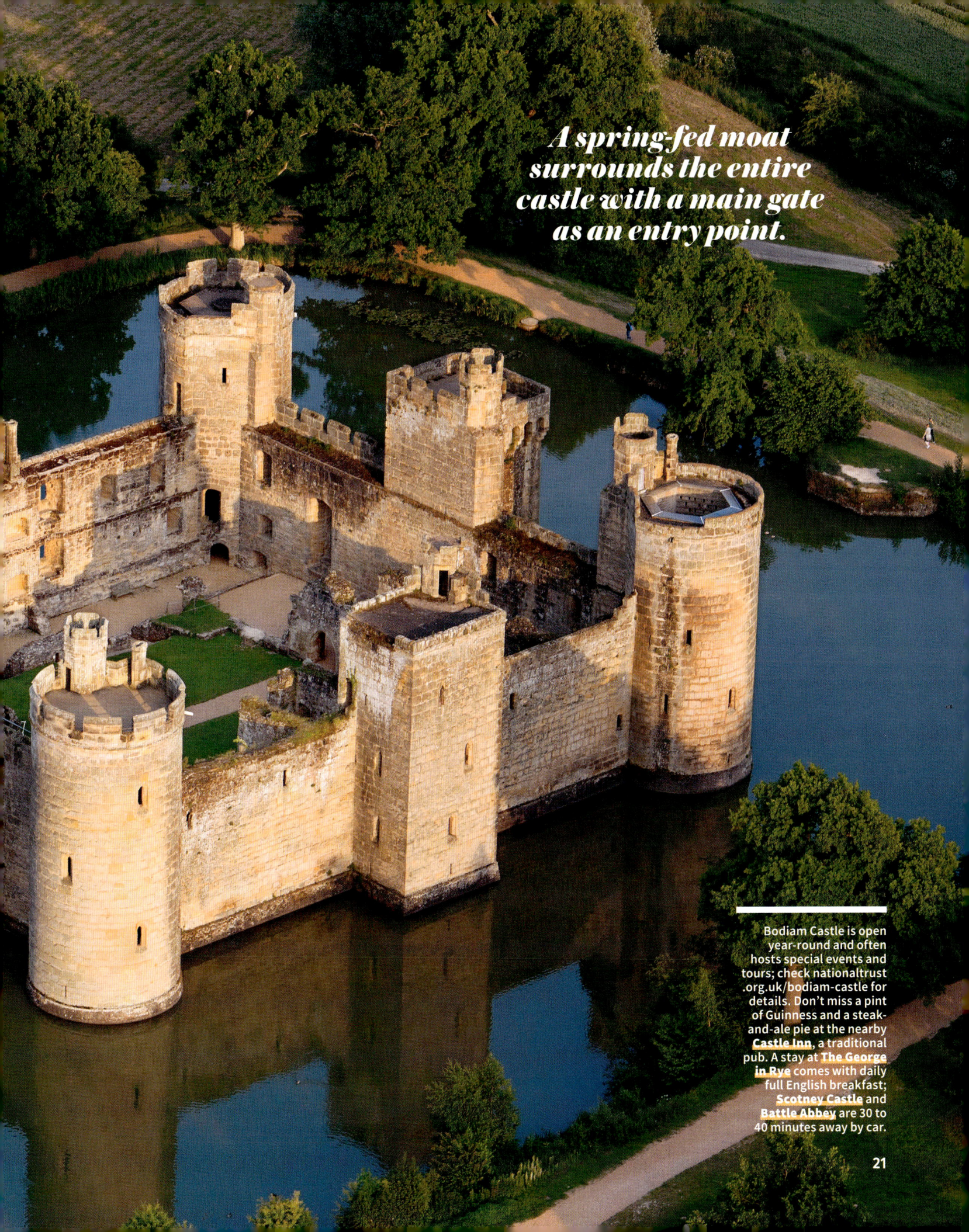

A spring-fed moat surrounds the entire castle with a main gate as an entry point.

Bodiam Castle is open year-round and often hosts special events and tours; check nationaltrust.org.uk/bodiam-castle for details. Don't miss a pint of Guinness and a steak-and-ale pie at the nearby **Castle Inn**, a traditional pub. A stay at **The George in Rye** comes with daily full English breakfast; **Scotney Castle** and **Battle Abbey** are 30 to 40 minutes away by car.

21

GREAT BRITAIN, IRELAND & SCANDINAVIA

Highclere Castle

HAMPSHIRE, ENGLAND

MANY VISITORS TO HIGHCLERE ARE already quite familiar with the estate, thanks to its time in the spotlight as the eponymous locale of the TV series and movie *Downton Abbey*.

The castle, dating back to the 1830s, is a relatively new addition to the land, but records indicate some structure among the acreage as far back as the year 749 A.D. A medieval palace followed in the 12th century, followed by a red brick Tudor house, but it wasn't until 1838 that the Carnarvon family commissioned building the grand Georgian castle. Sir Charles Barry—who had designed the Houses of Parliament—was brought in by the Third Earl of Carnarvon, and interior work took 40 years to fully complete.

At present, the Eighth Earl and Countess of Carnarvon spend part of the year in the castle and part nearby, but much like during the time depicted on the series, debt and taxes make upkeep difficult. So when the opportunity came to have *Downton* filmed somewhere, Lady Fiona, the Eighth Countess of Carnarvon, lobbied for Highclere.

At various times of the year, the castle is open for public tours, which help support the cost of maintaining the estate—everything from general upkeep to replacing 100-year-old mattresses. And as to how many bedrooms there are, Lady Fiona has actually lost count.

"I have come across rooms I didn't know were there, which is great," she once told PBS. "I came across a staircase I didn't know about."

The castle has a total of 300 rooms, including at least 61 bedrooms on the upper floors.

Between 60 and 150 people work on the estate, from the gardens to the tea room.

22 THE WORLD'S MOST AMAZING CASTLES

Highclere is open to the public throughout the year with special events in the spring and summer, but times are limited so check in advance. It takes about 90 minutes to drive from London to the castle; train service is also available from London's Paddington Station to Newbury with a 15-minute taxi ride to the estate. There are numerous lodging options in the region, including the luxurious **Cliveden House** and the expansive **Coworth Park**.

GREAT BRITAIN, IRELAND & SCANDINAVIA

Conwy Castle
CONWY, WALES

Nearby **Conwy** has numerous restaurants, pubs and cafes as well as hotels and B&Bs and is located about an hour's drive from both Liverpool and Manchester, England. The region is rich in culture and history; you may even hear some native Celtic Welsh being spoken. Local attractions include the well-preserved **Plas Mawr** Elizabethan town house, which dates back to 1585, and the 14th-century **Aberconwy House**.

Conwy Castle looms over the River Conwy in northwestern Wales, along the Irish Sea.

Conwy Castle is located in the region of Snowdonia, which sounds like a kingdom in Game of Thrones.

AS MEDIEVAL CASTLES GO, CONWY has impeccable credentials: eight round towers, two fortified gateways and walkable stone battlements offering panoramic views of the North Wales coastline.

Admirers can thank Edward I and master builder James of St. George for this exceptional 13th-century fortification, built on a massive rock in a small seaside town during the English king's conquest of Wales. Part of an "iron ring" of strongholds (others include Ruthin Castle and Caernarfon Castle) constructed to quash uprisings by the northern Welsh, this fortress holds visual treasures, both inside and out.

Pronounced "Conwee," the castle is the first thing visitors see when entering this charming town that time forgot. While most of Edward I's Welsh castles were designed in concentric circles, this one is a neat rectangle with almost identical towers, some of which can be climbed. This gives a great perspective on the design, with its Outer Ward and Inner Ward, home to private chambers, a chapel, the Kings Hall and the 125-foot, bow-shaped Great Hall.

Who called Conwy home? Edward I and his wife, Eleanor of Castille, lived here, as did their son, Edward II. More recently, the castle's significance earned it a spot as a UNESCO World Heritage Site.

GREAT BRITAIN, IRELAND & SCANDINAVIA

Edinburgh Castle

EDINBURGH, SCOTLAND

VISIBLE FROM ALMOST EVERYWHERE in Scotland's capital city, Edinburgh Castle is the quintessential fortress on a hill: dark, mysterious and brooding—and yet, when bathed in twilight's glow, simply magical.

Castle Rock, the volcanic outcropping on which the fortress sits 443 feet above sea level, has been occupied since the Bronze Age (850 B.C.). Royals took up residence in the 12th century, when the castle was built by David I, son of Saint Margaret of Scotland, who is honored in St Margaret's Chapel, the oldest building on the grounds.

Over the next six centuries, a host of royals called the castle home—notably, Mary Queen of Scots, who gave birth to James VI in her chambers in 1566 before abdicating two years later, and Charles I, who was the last monarch to reside here in 1633. Under siege numerous times over the centuries, the castle was captured by England's Edward I in 1296 and Edward III in 1334. The military has had a presence here since the 17th century, using the castle as a garrison, a prison and parade grounds.

Edinburgh Castle now attracts more than 2 million visitors annually and is part of a UNESCO site comprised of Edinburgh's Old and New towns. Today's travelers see the Royal Palace and Great Hall, Mons Meg (a massive 15th-century cannon), the Honours of Scotland (crown jewels) and the Stone of Destiny (the ancient Scottish coronation throne), a mystical icon of Scottish monarchy.

Check opening times and purchase tickets in advance at edinburghcastle.scot. Or opt for an **Explorer Pass**, which grants entry to Edinburgh Castle as well as more than 75 other Scottish attractions, including **Stirling Castle** and **Urquhart Castle**. Don't miss the firing of the **One O'Clock Gun** (yes, at 1 p.m. daily). Book a luxe room with castle views at **The Balmoral Hotel**, which dates to 1902.

Edinburgh's Ross Fountain is a jewel of 19th-century Scottish sculpture.

From its perch on Castle Rock, Edinburgh Castle inspires visitors to gaze upward.

27

GREAT BRITAIN, IRELAND & SCANDINAVIA

Dunnottar Castle
STONEHAVEN, SCOTLAND

WITH ITS JAGGED TOWERS JUTTING from a promontory high above the North Sea, Dunnottar Castle is a photographer favorite. History buffs (and fans of *Outlander*) know it for its role in the Jacobite rebellion, when its heavily fortified walls protected the Scottish crown jewels from Oliver Cromwell's invading armies following the coronation of Charles II. The jewel-encrusted crown, scepter and sword (the "Honours of Scotland") were smuggled into Dunnottar in sacks of wool and then, as Cromwell laid siege to the castle, lowered down the cliffs in a basket of seaweed. The last place to fly the Scottish flag, Dunnottar surrendered to Cromwell in May 1582, the jewels so well hidden in a nearby church that they remained there for nine years.

Visitors to the castle today will find a scene only slightly less dramatic, with massive stone walls, roofless towers, dank tunnels, a chapel and even a dungeon. (Most structures date from the 15th and 16th centuries, but King Donald of Scotland was attacked and killed by Vikings at Dunnottar in 934). The biggest attraction by far, however, is the view from the massive stone walls, with the sheer cliffs below and the sea pounding on three sides.

Historical records show that a fortress occupied this site possibly as early as 681 A.D.

The remains of this once-mighty fortress include a tower house, a chapel and a burial ground.

28 THE WORLD'S MOST AMAZING CASTLES

Be prepared for lots of steep stairs and dress warmly to ward off the blustery wind. Visiting hours are 9 a.m. to 6 p.m., April through September, and shorter and more variable in fall and winter. Check the website for closure notices. There are no advance ticket sales. Dunnottar is within walking and biking distance of Stonehaven, where **The Station Hotel** serves an excellent pub lunch, and a half-hour south of Aberdeen, where **The Chester Hotel** makes a perfect launch point.

GREAT BRITAIN, IRELAND & SCANDINAVIA

Kilkenny Castle

COLLEGEPARK, COUNTY KILKENNY, IRELAND

WITH ITS DIVERSE FUSION OF architectural styles, it seems only right that today, Kilkenny Castle endures as both a significant heritage site and a center for art and design.

Modern visitors can get their bearings in the landmark's foreboding medieval room, hunkered in the base of the South Tower. Here, arrow slits in the stone walls bear witness to the castle's original purpose as a defensive stronghold when it was completed in 1213 for William Marshal, the fourth earl of Pembroke.

As the tour progresses, features from various eras emerge— 16th-century foundation ruins, a massive 17th-century gateway and magnificent 19th-century interiors, from plush bedrooms to a drawing room and a library. Perhaps most impressive is the Picture Gallery Wing, flaunting an elaborate painted ceiling, a carved marble fireplace and portraits of the influential Butler family, who occupied the castle for almost six centuries.

This artful display is a harbinger of what's to come. In the basement, patrons can browse contemporary works in the Butler Gallery. And elsewhere on the grounds, the 18th-century Castle Yard—once stables and coach houses—is now home to the National Design & Craft Gallery, which hosts exhibitions, events and educational programs. Here at this popular landmark in the craft capital of Ireland, the past and present unite, and aesthetes can bask in an exquisite tribute to history and fine art.

The majestic castle has stood over the River Nore crossing for more than 900 years.

Other attractions at the castle include a tea room and 50 acres of public parkland. Grab lunch at the **Kilkenny Design Centre Restaurant and Foodhall**. After a full day of playing tourist, toast to your discoveries with a Castle Market mojito at **Statham's**. Turn in for the night at the **Butler House**, a 1770 Georgian mansion turned hotel. Tip: Be sure to leave room in your suitcase—a number of local shops sell Irish-made crafts.

Three of the four original 13th-century towers at Kilkenny Castle remain to this day.

GREAT BRITAIN, IRELAND & SCANDINAVIA

Blarney Castle

MONACNAPA, BLARNEY, COUNTY CORK, IRELAND

SOME PEOPLE WILL BEND OVER backward for an Instagram-worthy photo—and this medieval castle in County Cork is the place to do it, literally. Touristy? Absolutely. But once you're here, it's tough not to cave to tradition, lean back like a contortionist and kiss the hard, damp Blarney Stone in order to gain the gift of gab (or eloquence, as the castle promotes it).

So how did Blarney Castle, located a few miles north of the city of Cork, become the location of millions of stone-cold smooches? While the origin is uncertain, the leading theory maintains that it was a piece of the Stone of Destiny (upon which Scotland's kings were crowned), given by Robert the Bruce to Cormac McCarthy, King of Munster, to thank him for his aid during the Battle of Bannockburn in 1332.

What *is* known is that the stone was incorporated into the castle's battlements when it was built soon thereafter by the McCarthy clan and was bestowed with powers. (Some say a witch told Cormac of its magic; others claim that his descendant Dermot smooth-talked Queen Elizabeth I, earning the stone its fame). By the early 18th century, the castle and its storied stone had become legend: That's when the Oxford English Dictionary added the word "blarney" ("talk that aims to charm, flatter or persuade") to its pages.

The stone isn't the only attraction: Blarney is also home to dungeons, a cave and a lake.

A 1,500-acre garden hems Blarney Castle.

32 THE WORLD'S MOST AMAZING CASTLES

Blarney Castle is open Monday to Saturday; visit blarneycastle.ie to buy tickets ahead of time at a discount. To kiss the stone, you'll have to climb 128 narrow steps and then bend backward, grab onto a metal railing, and make upside-down lip contact (it's suspended 85 feet above the ground). Tip: Carry an antibacterial wipe to clean your lips afterward! Stay at **Longueville House**, a Georgian-era country house with an excellent restaurant and tranquil gardens.

GREAT BRITAIN, IRELAND & SCANDINAVIA

Dromoland Castle

COUNTY CLARE, IRELAND

WANT TO LIVE OUT YOUR IRISH-ROYALTY or *Game of Thrones* (minus the high stakes) fantasies? Dromoland Castle is the place. It dates to the 16th century and was once the home of the O'Brien family, the Kings of Thomond, whose lineage traces back to the High King of Ireland, Brian Boru. If its gray, Gothic-style stone walls could talk, they would tell of a storied past, which includes nearly being gambled away in a horse race in the 18th century, and threats of destruction by the IRA in the 1920s.

Transformed into a luxury hotel in 1962, the castle's main areas are frozen in time—life-size paintings of royalty line the walls; suits of armor guard the hallways. Afternoon tea is served in the main drawing room or the formal rose garden, followed by six-course meals under antique chandeliers in Earl of Thomond Restaurant. The baronial vibe continues in the 98 rooms and suites, fitted with four-poster beds, specially commissioned wall fabrics and bespoke furnishings. The two-story Honeymoon Suite is what happily-ever-after dreams are made of: It features a sitting room, a dining area, a bedroom and a Jacuzzi tub, all lodged in one of the castle's turrets.

The estate's grounds are a 450-acre emerald playground: Deer and pheasant pass through to drink from the lily pond. Guests can play a round at the golf course, fish for trout in the lake or unwind in the spa. At night, patrons gather in the Library Bar for Irish whiskey and lively sing-alongs. After a stay here, even cynics will acknowledge that fantasies can come to life.

The estate's 18-hole, par-72 golf course was designed by Ron Kirby and J.B. Carr.

34 THE WORLD'S MOST AMAZING CASTLES

The Dromoland grounds share the same designer as the Gardens of Versailles.

There's plenty to see and do at Dromoland, but other area attractions can also prove entertaining. The jaw-dropping **Cliffs of Moher** ranks as one of the most spectacular coastlines in the world, while scenic **Burren** offers views of green roads, karst limestone pavements and arctic and alpine flowers. If you'd rather stay at less expensive accommodations, **Carrygerry Country House** is a local favorite.

GREAT BRITAIN, IRELAND & SCANDINAVIA

Kronborg Castle

HELSINGØR, DENMARK

The marble-floored banquet hall was once the largest of its kind in Northern Europe.

THE RENAISSANCE CASTLE IMMORTALIZED AS HAMLET'S
Elsinore in William Shakespeare's eponymous tragedy, Kronborg can be found in Helsingor, Denmark, on the northeastern tip of the island of Zealand. Situated at the narrowest point of the Oresund—the 2.5-mile-wide sound between Denmark and Sweden—it's been burned to the ground and rebuilt, but its strategic location has offered protection and prestige to the nation for six centuries.

In its first lifetime, the castle was a basic fortress built by King Eric VII in the 1420s; dubbed Krogen, it controlled entrance to the Baltic Sea. King Frederick II, with the help of architects Flemings Hans Hendrik van Paesschen and Anthonis van Obbergen, transformed the stronghold into the spectacular castle we see today.

A UNESCO World Heritage Site, it's described by the Center as having "immense symbolic value to the Danish people," playing a "key role in the history of northern Europe in the 16th to 18th centuries."

After a fire destroyed large portions of the castle in 1629, King Christian IV swiftly built it back up to its former glory, but Kronborg was subsequently captured by the Swedes. In the late 18th century, Kronborg gave up its role as royal residence and instead, was used for army barracks. When the army left the castle in 1923, it was officially renovated and opened to the public. Today, visitors can purchase tickets to explore the rich history that lives within the walls of Kronborg Castle on their own, or through a selection of three guided tours.

Kronborg is open daily from May through September, and Tuesday through Sunday in the late fall, winter and early spring. Ticket pricing is seasonal. Fans of the Bard should plan their timing accordingly: Every August, *Hamlet* is performed, along with a selection of Shakespeare's greatest plays at the annual **Shakespeare Festival**. Laurence Olivier, Christopher Plummer and Jude Law have all played the titular character on the castle grounds, continuing a tradition that began over 200 years ago.

GREAT BRITAIN, IRELAND & SCANDINAVIA

Egeskov Castle

ISLE OF FUNEN, DENMARK

VISITORS GET A TRUE TASTE OF THE royal life at Egeskov Castle, one of the dwindling few that is still inhabited today (the count of Ahlefeldt-Laurvig-Bille lives there). First erected in 1554 by Frands Brockenhuus, the romantic Renaissance abode can be found on the island of Funen in Denmark.

Built as a defensive structure, the castle consists of two longhouses connected by a double wall so thick it includes hidden stairs and its own water supply, allowing those under siege to flee the first house and fight from the second. Notable defensive architecture includes a drawbridge that offered the only access to the house, and machicolations on the outer walls. Egeskov was sold by its original owners to Henrik Bille in 1784, and his descendants have owned it ever since. In more than 400 years it has seen little change, though Julius Ahlefeldt-Laurvig-Bille had an architect restore the structure, lifting the tower roofs, building a gatehouse and developing a model farm that is now a large, modern farm still in use today.

Step inside, and visitors can wander through a self-guided tour of the 15 accessible rooms (out of a total of 66), including a hunting room, bedrooms, a formal reception area and more. From the spires and turrets to the surrounding moat, guests will feel like they've stepped into a real-life fairy tale. That's only fitting: The castle claims the same birthplace as the father of fairy tales himself, Hans Christian Andersen.

The idyllic castle features 200 windows and 2,062 panes of glass.

Danish for "oak wood," it's said that an entire oak forest was felled for Egeskov's construction.

Egeskov is less than two hours by car from Copenhagen and well-worth a day trip—the 110-mile drive will get you to the front gate, where there's ample free parking and a camping site (free, but with a two-night maximum). Not just a historical relic, the family-friendly castle (open from May through October, with a Christmas market in December) comes alive with a large park, picnic areas, a treetop walk, games and a larch-tree maze designed by Count Claus Ahlefeldt.

GREAT BRITAIN, IRELAND & SCANDINAVIA

With several major roads passing through, those who controlled early Örebro controlled local trade routes.

Lasse-Maja, the notorious Swedish cross-dressing thief and memoirist, was jailed here.

From the **Children's Castle Tower** (where kids are encouraged to dress up in regal attire, take photos on the throne, lock their parents in dungeons, and shoot crossbows), to the haunted tales of ghosts and prisoners past, to dinner entertainment—the Örebro Castle truly has something to offer everyone. Centrally located for those already visiting the town, it's also an easy excursion from Stockholm, with trains departing the city at least once an hour. The total travel time is just under two hours.

Örebro Castle

ÖREBRO, SWEDEN

THE CITY OF ÖREBRO IS THE SIXTH- largest in Sweden, known best for its university, chamber orchestra, shopping center and 700-year-old weathered gray stone fortress.

Örebro Castle was first constructed in the 1300s as a stone house and defense tower, located on the northwestern part of the islet on the River Svartån. The tower itself was expanded in the 14th century, but it was under the House of Vasa in the 16th century that much of the castle as it is known today was erected. Though the castle has been the residence to the county governor for over 200 years, much of it remains open for the general public to explore and enjoy.

Beneath the surface, Örebro was not exactly the picture of fairy tales and princesses. More than just a defensive fortress, it also served as a dark prison over several centuries. With each expansion, new dungeons and torture chambers were added to the depths of the castle's ground floor. Famously, notorious Swedish thief Lasse-Maja was the sole survivor of Örebro's infamous caverns. No one knows how he escaped, but he was pardoned later in life by the crown prince.

The castle went through a sort of reverse renaissance toward the end of the 19th century, when it was restored to take on the older appearance of a Romanticist-style structure. To give the building medieval flair, white plaster was removed to reveal its original granite base, and the corner towers were given new domes.

MORE TO EXPLORE

Film Stars

Get to know these A-list castles that have all graced the silver screen.

Alnwick Castle

ALNWICK, ENGLAND

Alnwick Castle's impressive features—walled courtyards, 14th-century towers, Italianate state rooms, a moat—have made it a go-to location for the film and television industry. If you visit, sign up for the "Alnwick on Location Tour" to marvel at filming sites from TV's *Downton Abbey*, for which Alnwick served as Brancaster Castle for two Christmas specials of the wildly popular historical drama. You'll also get to see where scenes from *Robin Hood: Prince of Thieves* were shot and even transport yourself to the Hogwarts School of Witchcraft and Wizardry, as Alnwick had a magical starring role in the first two *Harry Potter* installments.

Enroll in a Broomstick Training session where Harry Potter learned to fly!

MORE TO EXPLORE

Bamburgh Castle
BAMBURGH, ENGLAND

The history of this immense coastal castle spans from prehistoric settlements to a Victorian restoration that concluded in 1905. More recently, it appeared in such films as *Elizabeth*, *Macbeth* and *Transformers: The Last Knight*. Modern visitors can explore the stronghold's 14 public rooms and see 2,000-plus artifacts, including armor, artwork and antique furniture.

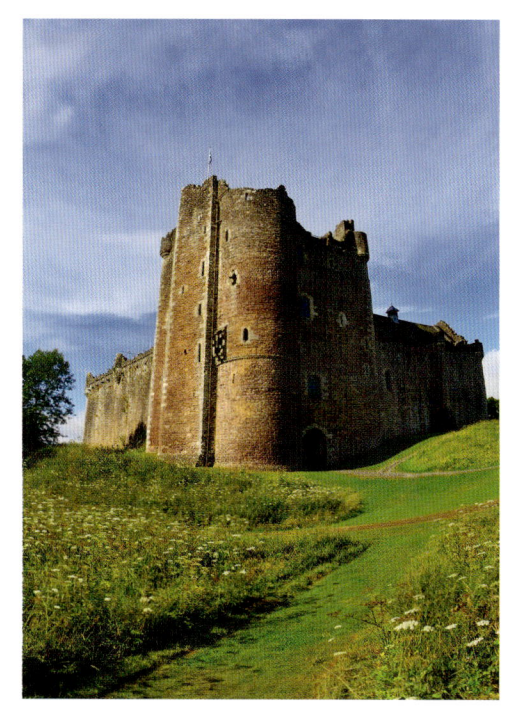

Doune Castle
DOUNE, SCOTLAND

This 14th-century castle has a flair for the dramatic—it was used in the filming of *Monty Python and the Holy Grail*; cast member Terry Jones narrates the audio tour for present-day visitors. Scenes from *Outlander* and *Outlaw King* were also shot here, and the tower famously appears as part of the Winterfell castle complex in season one of *Game of Thrones*.

Trim Castle
TRIM, COUNTY MEATH, IRELAND

The largest and best-preserved Anglo-Norman castle in Ireland, Trim Castle played the role of Carlisle Castle in the 1995 film *Braveheart*. Book a guided tour in advance (weekdays, November through February) to walk within the stronghold's stone walls and view a collection of medieval weaponry.

44 THE WORLD'S MOST AMAZING CASTLES

Eilean Donan Castle

KYLE OF LOCHALSH, SCOTLAND

Crowning an island in the Scottish Highlands, Eilean Donan Castle was opened to sightseers in 1955 after a modern restoration. More than a dozen films have used the 13th-century castle as a backdrop, including *Highlander*, *The World is Not Enough*, *Elizabeth: The Golden Age* and *Entrapment*.

Castle Howard

YORK, ENGLAND

Fans of both the 1981 adaptation of Evelyn Waugh's *Brideshead Revisited* and the 2008 version will likely recognize the stately exterior and grounds of Castle Howard, an elegant 18th-century mansion. The estate, which took more than 100 years to complete, has been appearing on screen since 1965's *Lady L* (starring Sophia Loren), with recent entries including the 2013 BBC adaptation of *Death Comes to Pemberley* and the 2016 ITV drama *Victoria*.

CHAPTER 2

GERMANY
& Austria

FAMOUS FOR THEIR LOFTY PERCHES THAT PIERCE THE CLOUDS, THESE COUNTRIES' SOARING SCHLOSSES HAVE INSPIRED COMPOSERS, POETS, NOVELISTS, FILMMAKERS AND EVEN THE LIKES OF WALT DISNEY.

German art historian Georg Dehio once called Eltz, located in Wierschem, Germany, the "quintessential castle."

47

GERMANY & AUSTRIA

Neuschwanstein Castle

SCHWANGAU, GERMANY

TRAVELERS TO THE GERMAN village of Schwangau are in for a treat: not one but two medieval-inspired castles, perched majestically in the Bavarian Alps.

Of course, Neuschwanstein—Walt Disney's inspiration for the fantastical Sleeping Beauty Castle—is the most famous, attracting 1.5 million visitors a year to its iconic blue turrets and soaring white walls. The vision of the reclusive King Ludwig II, the castle wouldn't be completed until 1892, six years after his suspicious death. Just weeks after his demise, his unfinished masterpiece opened to the public.

Of 200 planned rooms, only 14 are complete, but their over-the-top, Romanesque design vividly illustrates Ludwig's romantic—and unrealized—ideas about sovereign life. Stripped of his power following the Austro-Prussian War, the king nevertheless incorporated a two-story Byzantine throne room into his 65,000-square-foot schloss.

Nearby stands Hohenschwangau, Ludwig's childhood retreat. Dating to the 12th century, the castle was home to the Knights of Schwangau until 1535. Ludwig's father, Crown Prince Maximilian, purchased the ruined stronghold in 1832 and restored it to its original Gothic splendor, adorning it with murals of medieval poetry and legends.

All around both of these storied palaces, beautiful mountain scenery unfolds. Modern visitors soak in the panorama from Mary's Bridge, built by Maximilian for his queen and completed by Ludwig. As sightseers gaze across the Pöllat Gorge to the stunning silhouette of Neuschwanstein Castle, it's clear that Ludwig's intention to build a new castle "in the authentic style of the old German knights...from where one can enjoy a splendid view" was a smashing success.

48 THE WORLD'S MOST AMAZING CASTLES

Neuschwanstein is an example of "historicism," in which historical designs are copied—and perfected—using the latest craft skills.

GERMANY & AUSTRIA

Neuschwanstein Castle receives the most visitors of any castle in Germany and is one of the most popular tourist attractions in all of Europe.

> Purchase a combination Swan ticket, which includes **Hohenschwangau** and **Neuschwanstein** as well as the **Museum of the Bavarian Kings**; tickets must be purchased at the ticket center in the village of Hohenschwangau. Keep in mind: The castles are busiest between July and September, and tickets often sell out before noon. Base yourself in the quaint, 700-year-old town of **Fussen**, bustling with shops and restaurants.

50 THE WORLD'S MOST AMAZING CASTLES

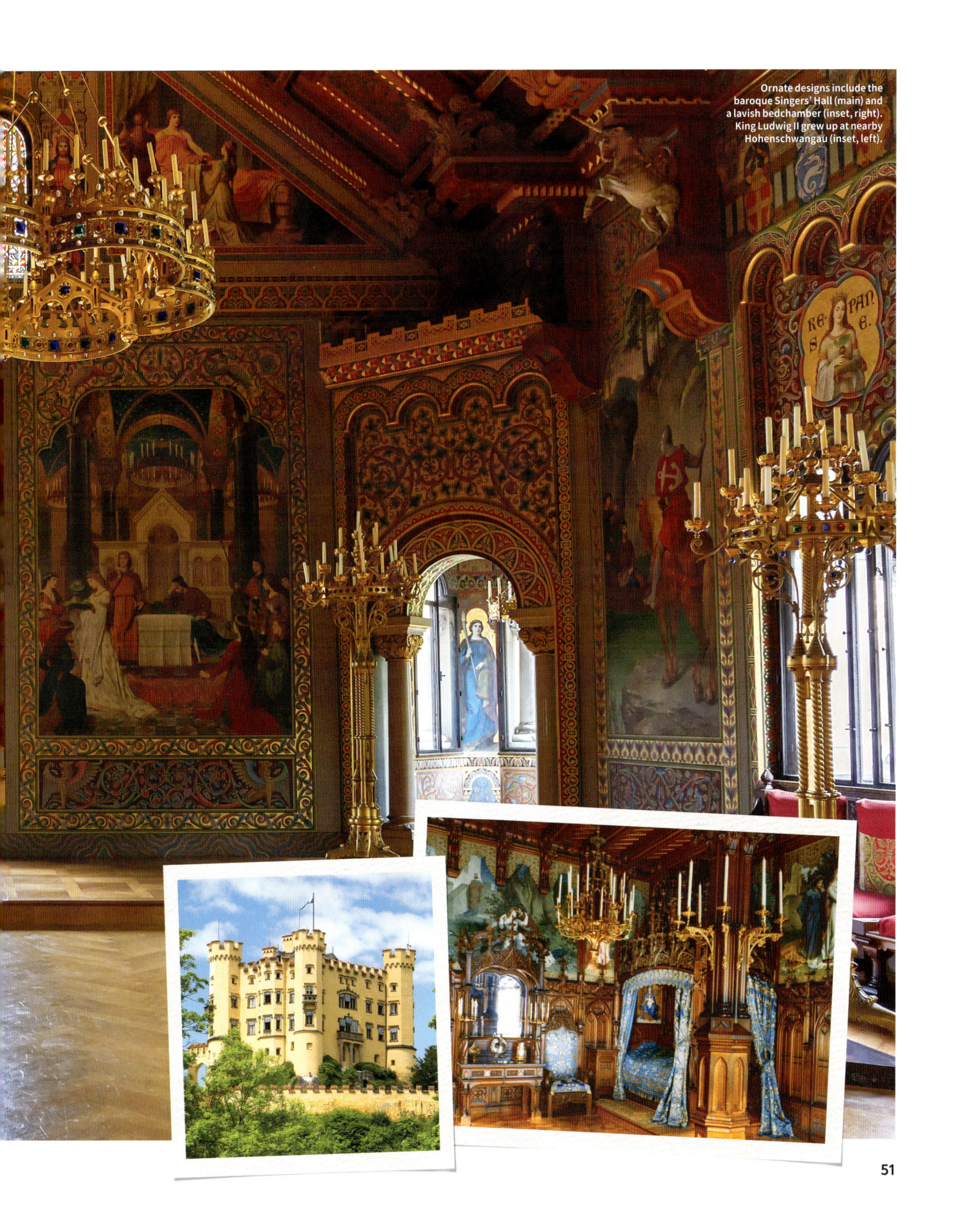

Ornate designs include the baroque Singers' Hall (main) and a lavish bedchamber (inset, right). King Ludwig II grew up at nearby Hohenschwangau (inset, left).

GERMANY & AUSTRIA

Tours of Lichtenstein Castle last 30 minutes and are in German. Allow extra time to try the **Lichtenstein Castle Ropes Course**, the castle's beer garden and the **Old Forester's Lodge** restaurant. The castle is an easy day trip from **Stuttgart**, the birthplace of the automobile (check out the city's **Mercedes-Benz and Porsche** museums). From Lichtenstein, continue another 2.5 hours to **Neuschwanstein Castle**.

52 THE WORLD'S MOST AMAZING CASTLES

Lichtenstein Castle

LICHTENSTEIN, GERMANY

Lichtenstein is appropriately named: It means "light-colored stone" in German.

THOUGH SMALL COMPARED TO the other great castles of Germany, Lichtenstein Castle drops jaws because of its rocky clifftop address —hovering over the Echaz Valley, 2,680 feet above sea level.

The lofty location made it a prime setting for a 14th-century fortress, which repelled every attack until it fell into disrepair in the 1500s. Centuries passed before the castle became a relatively modest hunting lodge. In 1840, the lodge was purchased by Count Wilhelm of Württemburg, who had much grander plans for the retreat.

Influenced by Wilhelm Hauff's novel *Lichtenstein*, the count re-created the castle in Gothic Revival style, crowning the original walls with battlements and designing palace chambers that epitomized the extravagant Late Romantic lifestyle.

Restorations between 1980 and 2002 allow modern visitors to view the castle's lavish spaces much as they would have appeared in their heyday. The tour makes its way through the chapel, the knight's hall, a garden, a courtyard and several castle rooms brimming with paintings, stained glass and medieval armor.

Affectionately known as "Württemberg's fairy-tale castle," this national monument stands tall as a charming tribute to the Romantic and Heroic styles. Drawing 100,000 visitors a year, it's proof that good things come in small packages.

Lichtenstein Castle is also often called Neuschwanstein's Little Brother, after Germany's most famous castle.

GERMANY & AUSTRIA

Heidelberg Castle seems to float over the city like a ghostly vision.

The palace is open every day; admission includes transport on a funicular train. Guided tours (required to tour the interior) are extra. During the summer, an artfully crumbling tower overlooking the river serves as an atmospheric stage for the city's annual **Heidelberg Castle Festival**; visit heidelberg.de for dates. Stay at the elegant **Europäischer Hof**, run by the same family since 1906.

Heidelberg Castle

HEIDELBERG, GERMANY

The red bricks of the ruins were plundered more than 200 years ago to build local homes.

THERE ARE MORE FAMOUS CASTLES IN THE world but perhaps no more famous castle *ruins* than those of Heidelberg Castle.

The oldest portions of the sprawling complex date to the 14th century, when King Rupert transformed what was once a small fortress into a palatial residence. Over the next 400 years, his descendants expanded the property, constructing massive buildings and spacious courtyards in a variety of architectural styles. Damaged by war, the castle was ravaged by a lightning fire in 1764 and sat vacant for more than 40 years. It was saved by a French count who, in 1810, took up residence within the ruins and successfully lobbied for the structure to be preserved.

Today, despite its scars, much of the castle is open for exploration. Highlights include the elaborately carved Baroque Elizabeth Gate (which Frederick V had constructed in a single night as a surprise birthday gift for his wife) and central courtyard, hemmed in by structures from the 14th to 17th centuries. Visitors gape at the Renaissance façades of Otto Henry and Frederick IV, the simple ruins of Rupert's original edifice and Frederick II's Glass Hall, with its arched Gothic walkways.

The castle rooms and hallways are filled with ancient statues, historic furnishings and, tucked below the Otto Henry Building, a 58,000-gallon wine cask (said to be the world's largest).

GERMANY & AUSTRIA

Set on its own island and surrounded by woodlands and lakes, Schwerin Castle was modeled after Château de Chambord in France.

The ceiling of the castle's neo-Gothic church is painted as a blue sky with golden stars.

Schwerin Castle

SCHWERIN, GERMANY

WHAT COULD COMPETE WITH A neo-Renaissance castle that boasts 635 rooms, a UNESCO bid and more than 800 years of history? Perhaps its immaculate 50-acre castle garden, a Baroque-style masterwork of flower beds, sculptures, terraces and covered walks.

Happily, the garden is free to enter, and the €8.50 (about $9.50) admission fee to the castle—rebuilt by Grand Duke Friedrich Franz II of Mecklenburg-Schwerin between 1847 and 1857—is well worth the price. Inside the original 16th-century walls, 19th-century ducal living is on grand display. Galleries, drawing rooms and throne apartments once used by the ducal family now showcase precious porcelain, medals, silver, jewelry, portraits, weapons and other artifacts. Most extraordinary is the throne room, featuring gilded doors and marble columns.

One of the last proper residence palaces in the country, Schwerin Castle was designed as a symbol of royal stability and power during a period of difficulty for German nobility. The reign of the grand dukes came to an end in 1918, and the castle became the property of the state. Today, in addition to functioning as a museum, Schwerin Castle serves as the seat of regional parliament.

The castle is even rumored to have a ghost—Little Peter, who has been haunting the palace's nooks and corners for centuries. Today's guests keep their eyes peeled for signs of his presence, including flickering lights and moving shadows. But of course, the castle's real-life sights, from soaring towers and golden domes to rich interiors and outstanding gardens, are more than enough to leave visitors amazed.

> Schwerin Castle's museum is closed on Mondays. Audio guides are available, or contact the museum in advance to arrange a tour led by an English-speaking guide. On-site food options include a greenhouse café (summer) and the **Schlosscafé** inside the castle (winter). Reserve a room at the circa-1901 **Niederländischer Hof** hotel. Alternately, excursions to Schwerin Castle are available on **Princess Cruises'** 11-day Scandinavia & Russia Cruises (from Berlin) itinerary.

GERMANY & AUSTRIA

Eltz Castle

WIERSCHEM, GERMANY

OF GERMANY'S STOIC RIDGETOP burgs, Eltz Castle stands out, thanks to its unusual history: It has been in the same family for all of its 850 long years.

Built to protect a trade route, the castle has stood on a large, 230-foot-high rock in the Eltzbach Valley since 1157, surviving wars, family feuds and shifting political alliances virtually intact. In fact, five centuries of building activity are reflected in the inner courtyard.

More than 500 exhibits—including gold, silver, coins, armor, jester masks, artwork and other curiosities—are on public display inside the castle's Armoury and Treasury, which has welcomed such famous visitors as poet Victor Hugo and American first ladies Lady Bird Johnson and Rosalynn Carter. Favorite rooms include the Knights Hall and a 15th-century medieval kitchen.

The castle's majestic exterior awes as well. Eight graceful towers hold court over a 740-acre nature reserve—a secluded scene that perfectly embodies the romantic illusion of the uncharted, untamed Middle Ages.

Eltz Castle is open seasonally, April to October. Make prior arrangements for a guided tour in English. Self-guided tours of the Armoury and Treasury are included in the entry fee. To avoid crowds, go before 11 a.m. or after 3 p.m. Refuel with schnitzel and beer at one of the castle's two self-service restaurants, **Unterschänke** and **Oberschänke**. Day trips to the castle are possible from **Frankfurt** and **Cologne**.

THE WORLD'S MOST AMAZING CASTLES

Inside Eltz Castle, many original household objects are still in place.

Eltz's Knights Hall features jesters' heads along the walls, representing free speech.

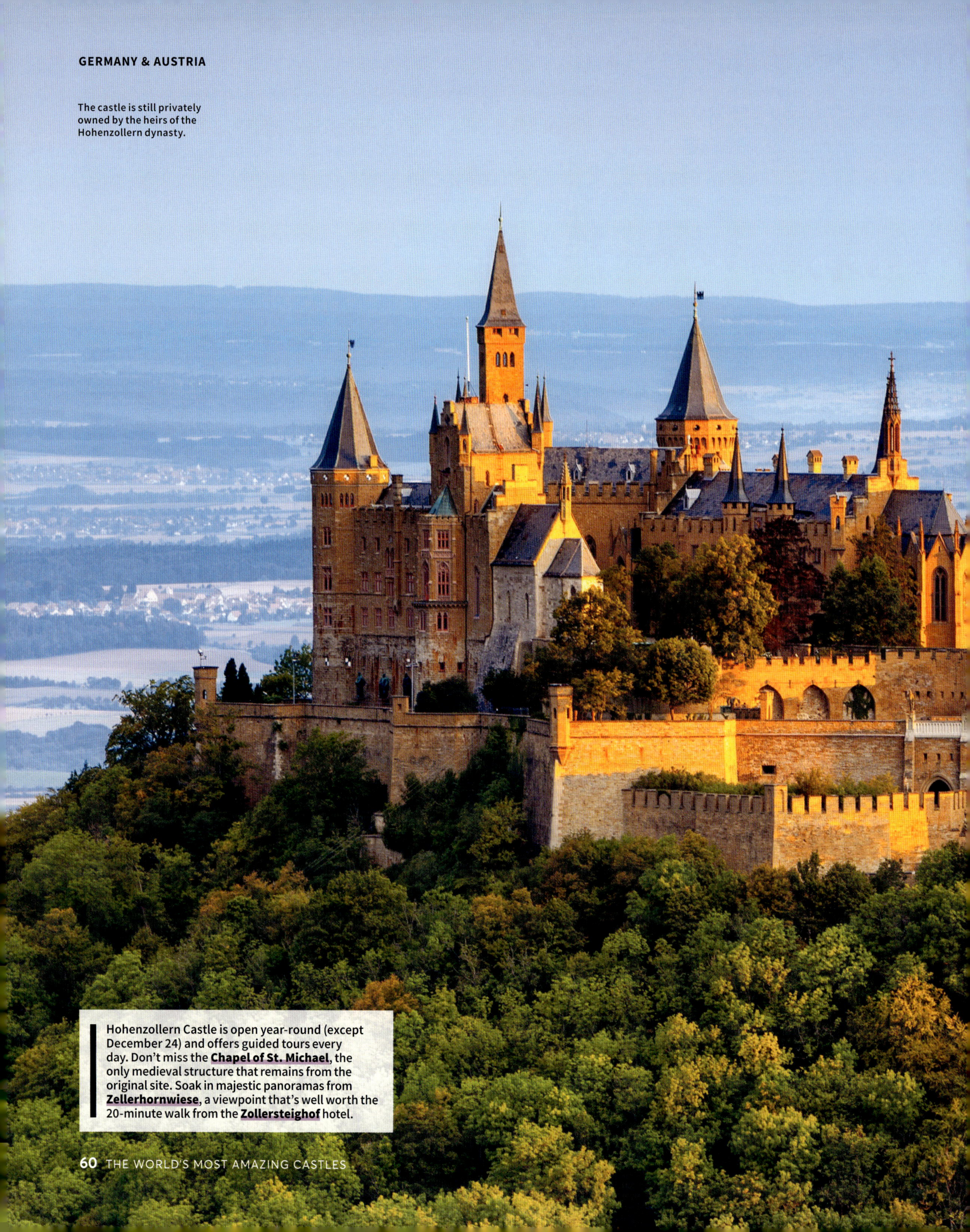

The castle is still privately owned by the heirs of the Hohenzollern dynasty.

Hohenzollern Castle is open year-round (except December 24) and offers guided tours every day. Don't miss the **Chapel of St. Michael**, the only medieval structure that remains from the original site. Soak in majestic panoramas from **Zellerhornwiese**, a viewpoint that's well worth the 20-minute walk from the **Zollersteighof** hotel.

Hohenzollern Castle

BISINGEN, GERMANY

Hohenzollern Castle has 140 rooms and draws more than 350,000 visitors each year.

A TOWERING HILLTOP FORTRESS floating 2,800 feet in the air, Hohenzollern Castle stands as a testament to persistence. First constructed in the 11th century, the lofty schloss has been entirely rebuilt three times.

Once the ancestral seat of counts and kings from the Hohenzollern dynasty, Burg Hohenzollern arises from the heart of Baden-Württemberg in the Swabian Alps. The first castle was destroyed in 1423 by war, then rebuilt, bigger and stronger, in 1454. It stood for three centuries, serving as a refuge during the Thirty Years' War, before falling into disrepair. After visiting the grounds in 1819, Prussia's King Frederick William IV vowed to restore the relic of his ancestors to its former glory, which he finally accomplished in 1867.

Inside, a gilded coffered ceiling overlooks exquisite inlaid floors, the Hohenzollern Crown sparkles with 142 rose-cut diamonds, and portraits of Prussian queens line the walls—which, if they could talk, would surely tell epic tales of the turmoil and triumph that have defined this millennium-old monument.

GERMANY & AUSTRIA

Artstetten Castle
ARTSTETTEN-PÖBRING, AUSTRIA

THE DETAILS SURROUNDING THE construction of the enchanting Artstetten Castle, located high on the Danube River near the Wachau Valley in Lower Austria, are murky. The first record of the medieval fortress can be found in the mid-13th century, and it proceeded to move through a succession of owners until Emperor Franz I acquired the schloss in 1823. Soon after, Archduke Carl Ludwig redesigned the house and, in 1889, gifted it to his son Archduke Franz Ferdinand of Austria. Ferdinand is credited for the extensive renovations the castle underwent in the late 19th and early 20th centuries, including electric wiring, an elevator, an English landscape garden and even a new wing. He's also credited for the worldwide relevance Artstetten continues to enjoy.

Today, the seven towers that cap Artstetten function as both museum and château: It serves as the year-round residence for current owner Anita Hohenberg and her family, plus there's a memorial to Ferdinand and his wife, Sophie, Duchess of Hohenberg, who were assassinated in Sarajevo in 1914, then buried in the crypt below the castle. The Archduke Franz Ferdinand Museum is housed in the castle's rooms as well, presenting ample photos, personal items, period furniture and even weaponry that bring to life the eventful story of his time at the castle and the start of World War I.

In late spring, glorious bursts of pink and white surround the castle as over 1,000 peony plants bloom.

Original owner Emperor Franz I had 14 other castles in his real estate portfolio.

The museum, family crypt and surrounding park are open daily from April 1 through November 1. Eighty-minute guided tours of the museum may be booked online or by phone, but must be done in advance. If you've got a group, you may be in luck: With advance notification, the museum can be opened during the off-season for parties of 20 or more. And if you're traveling with your pooch, bring Fido along—dogs are welcome at **Artstetten Castle!**

GERMANY & AUSTRIA

Hohenwerfen Castle

WERFEN, AUSTRIA

THE MEDIEVAL ROCK FORTRESS known as Hohenwerfen Castle, over 900 years old, sits on a precipice more than 2,000 feet high, overlooking the Austrian town of Werfen. The sights, sounds and refreshing air of the steep peak and surrounding Berchtesgaden Alps offer visitors a slice of life of nearly a millennia ago.

The fortress construction began in 1077, by order of the Archbishop after years of political unrest in Salzburg. Likely a simple wooden structure in its first iteration, Hohenwerfen continued to expand over the centuries. By the 16th century, peasants and farmers were revolting throughout the country, and the castle was plundered and destroyed. The damage was repaired under Archbishop Matthäus Lang, with new features including the Wallerturm watchtower and a hidden staircase.

From the 17th to the 18th century, the fortress was used predominantly as a prison and, after falling into disrepair under Bavarian rule in the early 1800s, it was restored to its former glory and expanded yet again until a fire destroyed the main building in 1931. The castle was briefly used as a military training center under Nazi rule, and then transitioned into Salzburg's police school until it was developed into a tourist attraction in 1987.

The castle has leaned greatly into tourist offerings to delight guests of any age. A daily birds of prey flight show put on by the historical regional falconry center, medieval feasts, interactive exhibits and daily castle tours are all on the docket—and everything (but the dining options) is included in the cost of a visitor's ticket.

The castle served as a backdrop in the 1968 Clint Eastwood film Where Eagles Dare.

Sitting just 26.7 miles apart, Hohenwerfen is a sister castle to the Hohensalzburg Fortress.

A transit-friendly destination, Hohenwerfen can be accessed through the **Werfen** station with direct connections to Salzburg. The 45-minute trip between Salzburg and Werfen runs every 30 minutes on the S-Bahn local rail service. From there, a 30-minute walk along a shady footpath takes you to the castle's door. Hours vary by day and season, so be sure to check their website before planning your trip. Dogs on leashes are welcome.

GERMANY & AUSTRIA

Listen for the circa 16th-century Salzburg Bell—a huge mechanical organ played three times daily from Palm Sunday to October 31.

Hohensalzburg is one of the largest medieval castles in Europe.

Hohensalzburg Castle

SALZBURG, AUSTRIA

AN INSTITUTION OF SALZBURG'S famous skyline, the 11th-century Fortress Hohensalzburg is instantly recognizable floating high above the city center. Built as a tribute to the pride and power of the Prince-Archbishops, the castle walls, though fortified many times over, only saw conflict once, during the German Peasants' War in 1525.

Hohensalzburg likely started out a basic wooden motte-and-bailey castle in its early days, but was greatly expanded in the ensuing centuries: In 1462, Prince-Archbishop Burkhard II von Weißpriach added the ring walls and towers. Around 1500, Archbishop Leonhard von Keutschach completed the basis of the fortress that can be seen today. During the Thirty Years' War (1618-1648), Archbishop Paris von Lodron added gunpowder stores and gatehouses to the fortress, and between the 16th and 17th centuries, the external bastions were added to protect against the potential threat of Turkish invasion.

It's been a prison (where, memorably, deposed Archbishop Wolf Dietrich von Raitenau died in 1617), a dungeon, a barracks and a storage depot, and though it was abandoned in 1861, it has since become a major tourist attraction and one of the best-preserved castles in Europe.

Guests can peek into the lives of the archbishops as they walk through the opulently furnished Golden Chamber, the princely bedchamber, the highly ornamented Chapel of Archbishop Leonhard von Keutschach, and the Golden Hall—used more for entertaining than defense.

The castle is open 365 days a year, including holidays. From **Midsummer's Eve** to a **Christmas Market**, special events pepper the schedule, so be sure to check if a festival is taking place during your visit. And while adventurers may want to hike from the Old City to the base of the castle, Austria's oldest funicular railway shuttles visitors up to the castle every 10 minutes for a small additional fee—and offers fantastic panoramic views of the region.

MORE TO EXPLORE

American Beauties

These 19th- and 20th-century stunners rival their European counterparts.

68 THE WORLD'S MOST AMAZING CASTLES

Around 10 million pounds of limestone were used to build the main house.

Biltmore Estate

ASHEVILLE, NORTH CAROLINA

Prepare to be wowed at Biltmore Estate—at 175,000 square feet, it's the largest home in America. George Vanderbilt (grandson of industrialist Cornelius Vanderbilt) and his wife, Edith, officially opened their French Renaissance-style château in 1895; its 250 rooms include 35 bedrooms, 43 bathrooms and 65 fireplaces. The gardens, designed by noted landscape architect Frederick Law Olmsted (of Central Park fame), are another spectacle. While on the grounds, visitors can rent bikes, take a carriage ride, go for hikes, try horseback riding and more. There's also an award-winning winery (which features complimentary tastings), numerous restaurants and three on-site hotels, so you can really take your time exploring all this grand estate has to offer.

MORE TO EXPLORE

Boldt Castle
ALEXANDRIA BAY, NEW YORK

Millionaire George C. Boldt, proprietor of NYC's Waldorf Astoria hotel, began building this six-story, 120-room Rhineland-style castle near the Canadian border in 1900 for his wife, Louise. But when she tragically died in 1904, he immediately stopped all construction. In 1977, the Thousand Islands Bridge Authority took the property over and restored it as an area attraction for visitors from May to October.

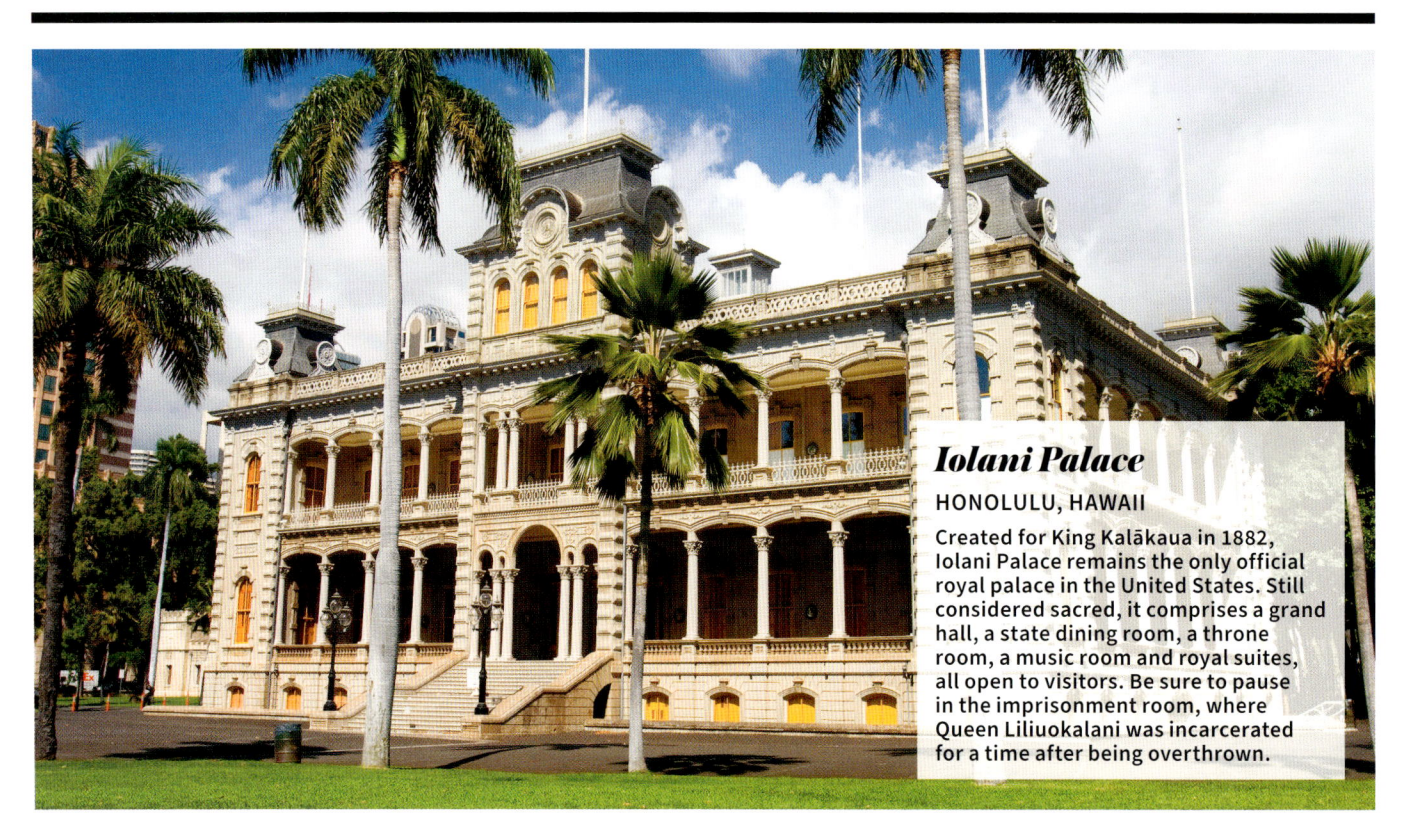

Iolani Palace
HONOLULU, HAWAII

Created for King Kalākaua in 1882, Iolani Palace remains the only official royal palace in the United States. Still considered sacred, it comprises a grand hall, a state dining room, a throne room, a music room and royal suites, all open to visitors. Be sure to pause in the imprisonment room, where Queen Liliuokalani was incarcerated for a time after being overthrown.

Thornewood Castle

LAKEWOOD, WASHINGTON

In 1907, financier Chester Thorne bought a 400-year-old Elizabethan manor in England, then had it systematically dismantled and shipped, piece by piece, to his lakefront property in Washington State, where it was used to construct the 54-room Thornewood Castle. Highlights of the home, which now operates as a bed and breakfast, include hand-painted stained glass from the 15th and 17th centuries, massive front doors crafted from 500-year-old English oak, and sunken gardens replete with sculpted fountains and statues.

Fonthill Castle

DOYLESTOWN, PENNSYLVANIA

Archaeologist, anthropologist, ceramist, scholar and antiquarian Henry Chapman Mercer built the castle from 1908 to 1912 using a mix of medieval, Gothic and Byzantine styles, calling it his "castle for the new world." Today, it's a museum and National Historic Landmark that receives more than 30,000 visitors a year who come to admire the building and its elaborate hand-crafted tiles.

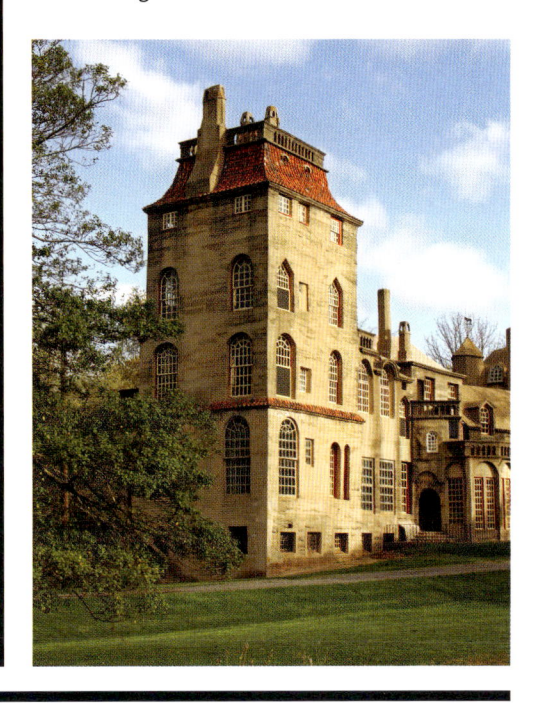

Hearst Castle

SAN SIMEON, CALIFORNIA

Almost a million visitors come every year to marvel at William Randolph Hearst's "Enchanted Hill." Completed in 1947, the estate is now managed by California State Parks, which lovingly preserve the 165 rooms and revered art collection. In addition to the outdoor Neptune Pool, there's also an indoor Roman Pool that holds 205,000 gallons of water, plus an airport and a wine cellar that was built with vaults to protect valuables.

CHAPTER 3

FRANCE
& Switzerland

FRANCE'S CHÂTEAUX ARE ARGUABLY THE MOST BEAUTIFUL IN THE WORLD. AND COLORFUL CHARACTERS, FROM JOAN OF ARC TO MARIE ANTOINETTE, BRING THEIR RICH HISTORIES TO LIFE.

France's Château de Sully-sur-Loire is part of a UNESCO site.

FRANCE & SWITZERLAND

Château de Chenonceau

CHENONCEAUX, FRANCE

MIRROR, MIRROR, ON THE WALL, what's the fairest castle of all? A powerful argument can be made for Château de Chenonceau, in the Loire Valley.

Built in the 16th century by French politician Thomas Bohier (apparently with tremendous input from his wife, Katherine Briçonnet), the château exudes a dreamy ambience that extends to its surroundings. The estate's Renaissance gardens were designed by King Henri II's mistress, Diane de Poitiers, to whom the king gifted the castle after seizing it in 1535. A study in the graceful aesthetics of geometry, the meticulously manicured grounds feature sculpted shrubbery, gracious flower beds and box trees trimmed to perfection. And the roses! Thousands of delicate iceberg roses cling to trellises on all sides. But wait: Diane de Poitiers' rival, Queen Catherine de Medici, also designed a garden here, set around a circular basin with views of the castle's west façade.

Step inside, and even more beauty awaits: Paintings by Rubens, Tintoretto, Veronese, van Dyck and others hang on walls lined with vibrant silk and edged in gilded wood. Perhaps it's apparent that women played a major role in the look of Chenonceau. A stroll here is magical, thanks to these historic ladies' eye for detail.

Château de Chenonceau's graceful arches and delicate turrets are splendidly reflected in the River Cher.

Château de Chenonceau is the most visited palace in the Loire Valley.

Château de Chenonceau is open every day; visit chenonceau.com to buy tickets ahead of time and avoid lines. The closest city to the castle is **Tours**, but you can also visit on a day trip from **Paris**, since it's just one hour away by high-speed train. Pack a picnic lunch to enjoy on the grounds (there are also two casual cafés and one fine-dining restaurant) or try a wine tasting in the historic cellar (from March to November). Stay at **Château de Perreux-Amboise**, which offers 11 contemporary rooms in a castle that dates to 1701.

FRANCE & SWITZERLAND

Château de Chambord

CHAMBORD, FRANCE

OF ALL THE SPECTACULAR CASTLES in the Loire Valley, Château de Chambord stands out for its sheer size—it's the largest of them all. Surrounded by a reflective moat and boasting 800 Italianate columns, 282 fireplaces, 77 staircases, 11 types of towers and three types of chimneys, the massive castle was listed by UNESCO in 1981.

Spring 2019 marked the castle's 500th anniversary: Construction began in 1519 as a hunting lodge for François I and took 28 years to complete. Leonardo da Vinci joined the court of François I in his last years and may have influenced many key design choices, such as the Ottoman-style roofline dotted with minarets. (Clos Lucé, his final home in nearby Amboise, makes a good companion visit; it also marked the 500th anniversary of his death in 2019.)

Inside the château, highlights include an open double-helix staircase of white marble almost certainly designed by da Vinci and spectacular vistas from the terraces and roof. The 18th-century furnishings of the château's final resident, the Comte de Chambord, include a lovely collection of tapestries.

Outside, the formal gardens reopened in 2017 after a $4 million restoration based on extensive historical research, so visitors can view them in much the same way as the counts of old did.

Château de Chambord is said to be the inspiration for the setting of Disney's *Beauty and the Beast*.

King Louis XIV enjoyed sojourns at Chambord with his court in the late 1600s.

Chambord is a 25-minute drive or taxi ride from the **Blois** train station. Shuttles run from the station from March 30 to early November. Alternately, **PARISCityVision** runs private tours directly from Paris. Or, if you can swing it, enjoy bedside views from the elegant **Relais de Chambord** hotel, which opened in spring 2018. French speakers can take a guided tour anytime, but English guides are available only from July through September. Grab a self-guided-tour map at the gate.

FRANCE & SWITZERLAND

The château got electricity after World War I, long before the villages below received it.

The French state confiscated the castle in 1919 after the signing of the Treaty of Versailles.

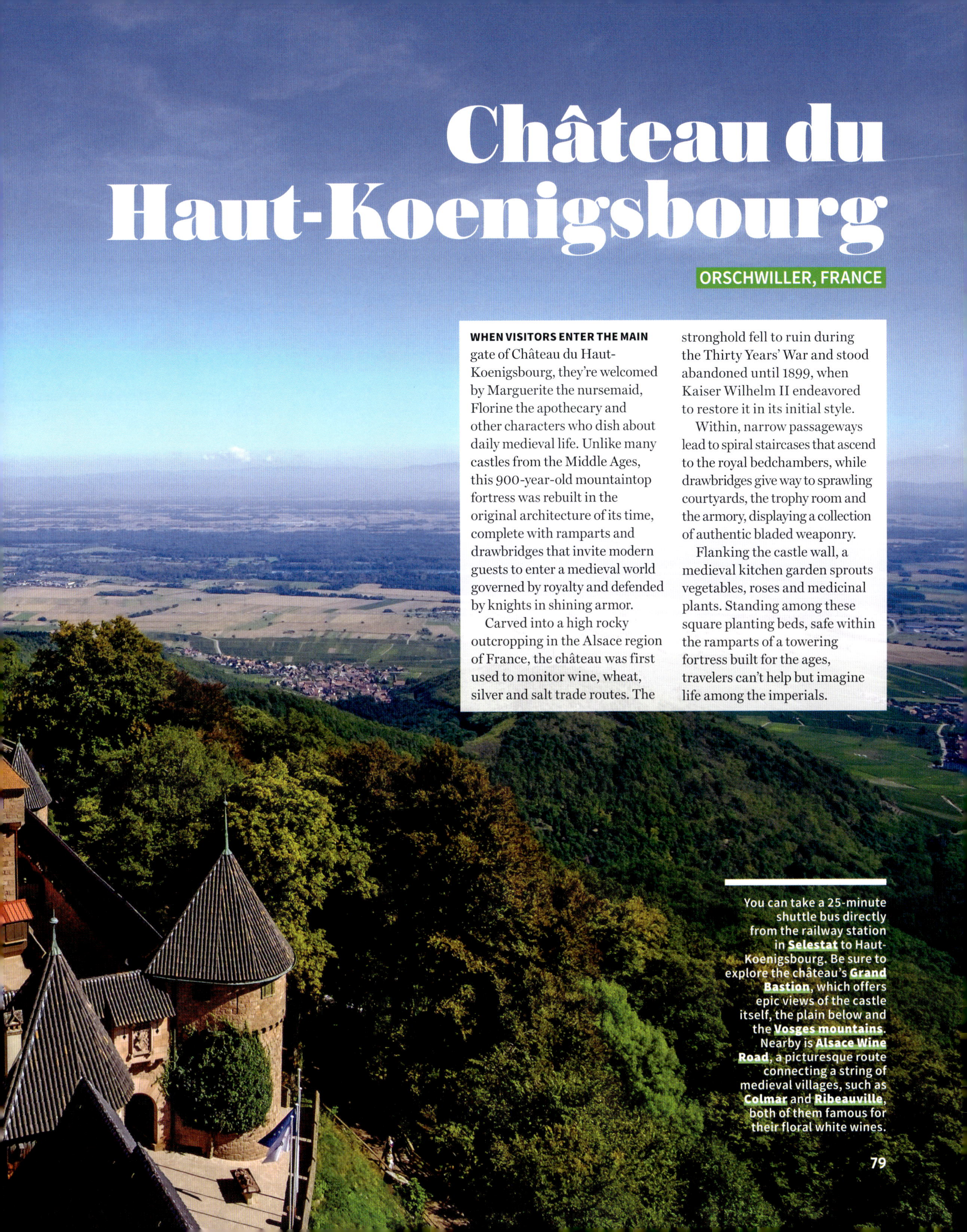

Château du Haut-Koenigsbourg

ORSCHWILLER, FRANCE

WHEN VISITORS ENTER THE MAIN gate of Château du Haut-Koenigsbourg, they're welcomed by Marguerite the nursemaid, Florine the apothecary and other characters who dish about daily medieval life. Unlike many castles from the Middle Ages, this 900-year-old mountaintop fortress was rebuilt in the original architecture of its time, complete with ramparts and drawbridges that invite modern guests to enter a medieval world governed by royalty and defended by knights in shining armor.

Carved into a high rocky outcropping in the Alsace region of France, the château was first used to monitor wine, wheat, silver and salt trade routes. The stronghold fell to ruin during the Thirty Years' War and stood abandoned until 1899, when Kaiser Wilhelm II endeavored to restore it in its initial style.

Within, narrow passageways lead to spiral staircases that ascend to the royal bedchambers, while drawbridges give way to sprawling courtyards, the trophy room and the armory, displaying a collection of authentic bladed weaponry.

Flanking the castle wall, a medieval kitchen garden sprouts vegetables, roses and medicinal plants. Standing among these square planting beds, safe within the ramparts of a towering fortress built for the ages, travelers can't help but imagine life among the imperials.

You can take a 25-minute shuttle bus directly from the railway station in **Selestat** to Haut-Koenigsbourg. Be sure to explore the château's **Grand Bastion**, which offers epic views of the castle itself, the plain below and the **Vosges mountains**. Nearby is **Alsace Wine Road**, a picturesque route connecting a string of medieval villages, such as **Colmar** and **Ribeauville**, both of them famous for their floral white wines.

FRANCE & SWITZERLAND

The master bedroom was actually never used before the castle became a museum.

Château de Pierrefonds

PIERREFONDS, FRANCE

WITH ITS "RAPUNZEL"-STYLE TOWERS, arched gateways and ghostly gargoyles, Château de Pierrefonds looks like a castle straight out of Arthurian legend. In fact, the château stood in for Camelot on the TV drama series *Merlin*.

A modern-day outing to this Picardy-area landmark is no less fanciful. Guests can walk along the crenellated parapet, stroll through echoing corridors and gawk at the decadent interior adorned with ornate Renaissance-style paneling, imposing marble sculptures and colorful Art Nouveau wall coverings.

Built in the 14th century by Louis I, Duke of Orleans, the château was destroyed in the 17th century and left in ruins for 200 years, then reconstructed during the Romantic period by order of Napoleon III. The re-creation allowed Napoleon's chosen architect, Eugène Viollet-le-Duc, to meld the most dramatic aspects of medieval architecture with more modern aesthetic ideas to create an idealized castle. The result: a grandiose "pleasure palace" that took more than 20 years to build and became known as the emperor's "folly."

Of course, what may have been viewed as foolishness in the past is now celebrated on lists of France's best castles. Perhaps those who venture through its gates aren't so much seeking historical accuracy as wise wizards and swords in stones.

The château is now a national monument managed by Le Centre des Monuments Nationaux.

Just 50 miles and 1.5 hours by car from **Paris** (there is no train stop nearby), the château is doable as a day trip, but leave plenty of time to explore the red-roofed village of **Pierrefonds** and its serene lakeside setting. Linger at the 13th-century Gothic **Church of Saint-Sulpice**, then savor lunch at the **Restaurant Auberge Aux Bles d'Or Pierrefonds**, housed in a historic mill. A cocktail on the outside deck at **L'embarcadere Pierrefonds** makes a nice finish.

FRANCE & SWITZERLAND

Château de Villandry

VILLANDRY, FRANCE

DURING THE RENAISSANCE, AS interest in classical art and literature surged, medieval strongholds took on a new character. Fortresses became ornamental castles. Kitchen gardens morphed into sprawling decorative parks. And defensive walls were transformed into scenic overlooks. This evolution was especially true at Château de Villandry, the last of the great Loire Valley châteaux.

Jean Le Breton, finance minister for King François I, acquired the property in 1532 and built his grand château from scratch—save the 12th-century keep (central tower) of the old fortress. Drawing on his experience in overseeing the construction of Château de Chambord for François I, Le Breton imbued his own estate with Renaissance symmetry and style: steep rooflines, sculpted dormer windows and ornate rectangular columns.

Even more impressive were the six landscaped gardens—15 neat acres of geometric flower beds, fountains, hedges, groves, terraces, vines and color-coordinated vegetable patches.

When new owners took over in 1754, the castle and its gardens lost much of their Renaissance charm. But they were blessedly restored in the 20th century by Dr. Joachim Carvallo and his wife, Ann Coleman. In 1920, the Carvallo family opened the château to the public, which has been inspired by its grace for almost 100 years. As visitors walk through the estate, it's clear that here, Renaissance fashion rules over medieval function.

Château de Villandry was one of the first Loire Valley castles to open for public visitation.

An expert team of 10 gardeners tend daily to the gorgeous grounds.

A full-price ticket to Château de Villandry grants discounted entry to numerous other historic attractions in the area, including **Château d'Azay-le-Rideau**, **Château de Langeais** and **Château de l'Aulee**'s wine cellar. Indulge in traditional cuisine at **L'Étape Gourmande**, housed on a 17th-century farm, and sleep in comfort at **Hotel & Spa La Marine de Loire**, which has its own garden, spa and Turkish bath.

FRANCE & SWITZERLAND

Château de Sully-sur-Loire

SULLY-SUR-LOIRE, FRANCE

CHÂTEAU DE SULLY-SUR-LOIRE—located at the eastern gateway of the Loire Châteaux region—is not only an impressive sight, it also boasts a stellar list of historic houseguests: No less than a king (Louis XIV), a writer (Voltaire) and a saint (Joan of Arc) have all spent the night here. Constructed over several periods throughout three centuries, this medieval fortress takes its name from its celebrated owners, the 14th-century Lord of Sully (Guy de la Trémoille) and the 17th-century Duke of Sully (Maximilien de Bethune), as well as its location on the left bank of the Loire River.

While it was designed primarily as a defensive castle (yes, there's a moat), this château also impresses visitors with its cylindrical turreted towers and vibrant early-Renaissance architecture as well as the mostly 17th- and 18th-century furnishings—think painted ceilings, deep-red walls and a massive cornflower-blue canopy bed—of its residential Petit Château.

On the 90-minute guided tour, visitors explore more than a dozen art- and antiques-filled rooms and view the 10 tapestries of the 17th-century Psyche curtain, which depicts the Greek goddess of the soul. Other spots to check out include the keep (one of the oldest sections of the château), the parapet walk, the dungeon, and the tomb, where the Duke of Sully and his second wife lie in repose.

Joan of Arc stayed at Sully twice to visit with the future King Charles VII, whom she fought to see crowned.

The château was built to guard a location where the Loire River could be crossed.

84 THE WORLD'S MOST AMAZING CASTLES

Located 81 miles from **Paris**, Château de Sully-sur-Loire is open every day in July and August, and Tuesday to Sunday the rest of the year (except January, when it's closed). Visit chateau-sully.com for hours and details. Unlike some other notable French châteaux that are surrounded by gardens, this one is ringed by water and located in the middle of the town of **Sully-sur-Loire**. This offers additional opportunities for sightseeing, shopping and dining on local **Loire Valley** specialties such as goat cheese, wild boar and *rillettes* (similar to pâté). Stay the night at **Hotel Burgevin**, a charming 16-room property nearby.

FRANCE & SWITZERLAND

Palace of Versailles

VERSAILLES, FRANCE

Order, balance and symmetry rule the day throughout the buildings and gardens.

THE LEGEND GOES THAT WHEN MARIE ANTOINETTE, QUEEN OF France from 1755 to 1793, was told the people had no bread, she flippantly replied, "Let them eat cake." It's doubtful the famous monarch really uttered these words, but the rumor still echoes through the lavish halls of Versailles, the ultimate homage to French royal power.

Located 10 miles outside Paris, the palace began as a hunting lodge for King Louis XIII. In 1682, his son, Louis XIV, relocated the country's government and court there. As he and the succeeding kings of the *ancien régime* excessively enhanced Versailles, the French Revolutionary movement fomented, eventually resulting in the beheadings of Marie Antoinette and her husband, Louis XVI.

Today, rather than incite, the palace's indulgences delight its crush of visitors. Each year, more than 7 million people ogle their way through Versailles' yawning Gallery of Great Battles, prestigious King's State Apartments, ornate Hall of Mirrors and gilded Queen's Bedchamber, where Marie-Antoinette delivered her first, long-awaited child—purportedly before a crowded room full of nosy spectators.

FRANCE & SWITZERLAND

The Palace of Versailles is open daily except Monday; take the 30-minute RER C commuter-train line from Paris. If you can, avoid weekends and Tuesdays, when Paris museums are closed. Consider springing for the Paris Museum Pass, which grants access to Versailles along with many other area monuments, including the Louvre, the Arc de Triomphe and the Musée d'Orsay.

88 THE WORLD'S MOST AMAZING CASTLES

The historic Treaty of Versailles, which ended World War I, was signed in 1919 at the palace. Many of the bedrooms feature lavish textiles (inset).

FRANCE & SWITZERLAND

Château de Chaumont-sur-Loire

CHAUMONT-SUR-LOIRE, FRANCE

THE YEAR 1559 WAS A TUMULTUOUS one for French noblewoman Diane de Poitiers. Her lover, King Henri II, was mortally wounded in a joust, and his queen, Catherine de Medici, evicted de Poitiers from Château de Chenonceau, the castle he had given his "favorite." Her consolation prize: Château de Chaumont-sur-Loire, a Renaissance-style castle perched 130 feet above the Loire River.

First erected as a fortress in the year 1000, the château was rebuilt in the 1400s. But credit for its current layout, furnishings and landscaping goes to Princess Amédée de Broglie. Far from seeing the castle as second choice, she fell in love with the estate at first sight and bought it in 1875 at the age of just 17. The property was the scene of her extravagant balls and banquets until 1938, when it was ceded to the state.

Visitors can view 19th-century portraits of the king's rival paramours: Catherine de Medici, in her eponymous room, and Diane de Poitiers, in the council chamber. Other notable features: a spiral grand staircase, the King's Room (and the world's greatest medallion collection) and the 19th-century stables, once among the finest in Europe.

The château also inspires travelers with its contemporary art and 80-acre garden. With masterpieces from medieval to modern, it's obvious that this French landmark has many stories to tell.

Princess de Broglie established a pet cemetery on the grounds, where graves still bear poems to her beloved animals.

Château de Chaumont-sur-Loire has been receiving guests for centuries.

April through October is the optimal time to visit Château de Chaumont-sur-Loire, when the **International Garden Festival** is underway. Refuel at one of six on-site restaurants and cafés, including **Le Grand Velum**, serving local, organic fare. Dating to 1880, **Les Hauts de Chaumont** is an adorable B&B that puts guests within arm's reach of Château de Chaumont as well as the Loire Valley's other top castles: **Chenonceau**, **Chambord** and **Cheverny**.

FRANCE & SWITZERLAND

Gruyères Castle

GRUYÈRES, FRIBOURG, SWITZERLAND

THE GRUYÈRES CASTLE (YES, LIKE the cheese) is situated in the Alpine hills of the picturesque Swiss town of the same name. And while the famous cheese factory—and taste-bud-rivaling chocolate factory—are the town's best-known tourist stops (if they're not on your to-visit list yet, they should be), the opulent medieval castle is worth a stop for those passing through.

Gruyères Castle, a Swiss heritage site, was built between 1270 and 1282 as property of the Counts of Gruyères, a noble family in the region, until the bankruptcy of Count Michel in 1554. After changing hands through the centuries, the castle was turned into a museum by the Canton of Fribourg and the grandiose space opened to the public in 1938.

Since 1993, a foundation has been responsible for managing and conserving the château, as well as sharing both the castle's awe-inspiring architecture and prized possessions (including three capes of the Order of the Golden Fleece and the stunning medieval-era stained glass windows), and its expansive art collection (landscapes by Jean-Baptiste-Camille Corot and Barthélemy Menn adorn the walls), with the touring public. Visitors should take pause as they pass the grand lattice windows to take in stunning verdant views of the countryside.

You can meet storytellers in medieval attire at this 13th-century stronghold in the foothills of the Alps. Afterward, taste the product of master cheesemakers at La Maison du Gruyère.

92 THE WORLD'S MOST AMAZING CASTLES

Behind the château, you'll find French gardens and showstopping village views.

Open daily year-round; while there is no official guided tour, special accommodations can be made upon request. Otherwise, explore the castle with the aid of a handout guide (available in 12 languages), and a 20-minute multimedia show; both are included with the price of entry. Local accommodations are plentiful for a cobblestone town of just over 2,000—for an intimate experience try the **La Ferme du Bourgoz**, walkable to both the train station and old village.

FRANCE & SWITZERLAND

The complex includes 25 buildings and three courtyards, protected by two circular walls.

> *The romantic aesthetics of Chillon have inspired many artists and authors, including Lord Byron and Victor Hugo.*

> Buy tickets to the castle online up to three months in advance at **chillon.ch** or in person upon arrival. Guided tours are available in 10 different languages and must be booked at least two days in advance. Be sure to stop for a picnic—or even a swim—on the beach next to the castle, where there are showers and toilets available for public use.

94 THE WORLD'S MOST AMAZING CASTLES

Chillon Castle

VEYTAUX, VAUD, SWITZERLAND

PERCHED ATOP A ROCKY OUTCROP on the far western end of Lake Geneva is the Château de Chillon. Situated on the island of Chillon, it is one of the most-visited castles not just in Switzerland, but in all of Europe. More than 400,000 tourists are drawn to its breathtaking views of the Lake, and storybook-style towers, courtyards and latticed windows.

Though first built around the 10th century by the rulers of Savoy, excavations have found objects on its land dating all the way back to Roman times, leading archaeologists to believe it was a military site long before the first tower was fortified. From its strategic spot, Savoy controlled trade and traffic through the region. While the Bernese commandeered the castle in the 16th century, Chillon's location had lost much of its significance just a few centuries later, and was relegated to storage space until its resurgence as a tourist gold mine in the 19th century. The location of Chillon is well-suited to day-trippers from nearby Geneva or the many popular ski resorts in the Alps.

When touring the castle today, guests can enjoy recreations of many rooms, including the grand bedroom, hall and cave stores. Visitors can also tour great halls, courtyards and publicly viewable bedrooms. One of the oldest is the 13th century *Camera domini* (the lord's bedroom) which was, for centuries, occupied by the sitting counts and dukes of Savoy, and is decorated with multiple magnificent 14th-century medieval murals.

FRANCE & SWITZERLAND

Open Tuesday through Sunday, mid-May through late October, tickets can be purchased for the castle museum on site. The **Thun Railway Station**, via connecting buses, and the boat to Oberhofen offer easy access to the castle. Rooms can be rented out on premises for weddings and celebrations. Dine on the lake at the **Restaurant Schloss Oberhofen** and don't miss the garden inside the castle complex and the landscaped park adjacent to it—both of which can be visited for free.

Oberhofen Castle

OBERHOFEN, SWITZERLAND

Impressive murals in the 15th-century chapel were commissioned by the Scharnachtal family.

SEATED ON THE SHORES OF LAKE
Thun, near Bern in Switzerland, Oberhofen Castle towers over the waters. Embodying the spirit of the picturesque country, the fantastical vision of one tower seemingly rising out of the lake itself only adds to the structure's beauty and mystery.

A Swiss heritage site of national significance, the central fortress keep—measuring just 36 feet by 41 feet—was likely built back in the early 13th century. The rest of the castle was developed around the keep in the ensuing centuries. As the castle passed through many hands, both public and private, a chapel was added to the first floor in 1473, and the majority of the castle's upgrades occurred between 1652 and 1798, transforming the once simple keep into an impressive estate.

Kept as a residence until the mid-20th century, museum visitors can explore life between the 16th and 19th centuries, seamlessly traveling through time as they stop to admire the Knights Hall, the summer hall and the neo-Gothic dining room. On the ground floor, guests can enter the dining room where the noble family in residence would eat, and the bailiff-era dungeon. After walking the stairs to the second floor, visitors take in the servants' living quarters, and at the top of the old keep is the smoking room of Albert de Pourtalès. Not to be missed, the castle's highest point offers breathtaking views of the lake and mountains below.

Get a scenic view of the castle from the deck of a pleasure boat on Lake Thun.

MORE TO EXPLORE

98 THE WORLD'S MOST AMAZING CASTLES

Southern Stunners

South America, Australia and Africa lay claim to their own impressive estates, inspired by the Old World.

Inside, you can admire exhibits of paintings, photography and sculptures.

Wulff Castle
VIÑA DEL MAR, CHILE

In 1917, a German émigré businessman named Gustavo Adolfo Wulff Mowle hired an architect to transform his existing home on a rocky promontory overlooking the Pacific Ocean into a striking edifice that resembled the castles of his homeland. The end result, with its stone walls, Gothic towers, spire, crenellated roof and arched windows, wouldn't look out of place in Bavaria (or Disneyworld). The interior is equally dramatic: A hallway has a partial glass floor that allows you to peer down at the waves as they crash on the rocks below. Now, this Instagram-friendly landmark is an exposition space and tourist attraction with an observation deck that offers expansive views of the sea and the cityscape.

MORE TO EXPLORE

Government House
SYDNEY, AUSTRALIA

This two-story Gothic Revival castle is the home of the Honourable Margaret Beazley, the current governor of New South Wales, and her husband. Designed by Edward Blore, an architect who also worked with William IV and Queen Victoria and on Buckingham Palace and Windsor Castle, the building was constructed between 1836 and 1845. Standout flourishes include its castellated towers and intricately hand-painted stencil ceilings. The 12-acre garden offers unique views of Farm Cove bay and the Sydney Opera House.

Ilha Fiscal
GUANABARA BAY, BRAZIL

Inaugurated in April, 1889, this lime-green neo-Gothic castle was initially the home of the Brazilian Custom Service. It hosted the final party of the empire before Brazil was declared a republic. Inside find gorgeous hardwood mosaic floors, impressive stained glass and a regal Ceremonial Room now used for formal navy events.

Fasil Ghebbi Castle
GONDAR, ETHIOPIA

This enchanting complex of castles and official buildings surrounded by a half-mile-long wall was built in the 17th century by the Emperor Fasil, who made Gondar the seat of government power. Inscribed as a UNESCO World Heritage Site in 1979, it's a very early example of multiculturalism, reflecting Orthodox, Hindu and Arab influences. It's open to visitors—or go to zamaniproject.org for a 3D virtual tour.

Duwisib Castle

SOUTHERN NAMIB REGION, NAMIBIA

It looks like a siege-proof medieval fortress rising from the semi-arid hills, but it was in fact built not by a king, but by a German army officer, Captain Hans Heinrich von Wolf, as a family home for his bride. Construction of the 22-room building was completed in 1908, but von Wolf was killed in World War I and his wife never returned.

Palacio de Aguas Corrientes

BUENOS AIRES, ARGENTINA

This French Renaissance palace opened in 1894 and housed the city's water system (its name translates to the Palace of Running Water). The three top floors contained 12 tanks that stored about 72,000 tons of drinkable water. Taking up an entire block, it still functions as an office for the city water company and a small museum. Beneath its tin mansard roof lies a fascinating façade that's impressively adorned with 300,000 terra-cotta ceramic tiles imported from Britain and Belgium.

Portugal's Pena Palace headlines the cultural landscape of the Sintra UNESCO site.

CHAPTER 4

Southern EUROPE

FROM PORTUGAL'S ECCENTRIC PALACES AND SPAIN'S MOORISH FORTRESSES TO ITALY'S SEASIDE CITADELS, THESE CASTLES BLEND MAJESTIC ARCHITECTURE WITH A BALMY MEDITERRANEAN CLIMATE.

SOUTHERN EUROPE

Alcazar of Segovia

SEGOVIA, SPAIN

Skip the guided tour (unless you're fluent in Spanish) and just purchase the full-entry pass, which grants access to the palace rooms, Artillery Museum and Tower of Juan II. Tickets must be bought same-day, and audio guides are available to rent in 12 languages, including English. Don't miss other historical sights nearby, including an ancient Roman **Aqueduct** and the 16th-century **Segovia Cathedral**. Sleep like a celebrity at **Hotel Real Segovia**, which has hosted Old Hollywood film stars like Sophia Loren and Joan Fontaine.

The castle gets its name from the Arabic word *al-qasr*, which translates to "fortress."

Along with Neuschwanstein in Germany, Alcazar of Segovia is said to have inspired Walt Disney's iconic theme-park castles.

WITH ITS SECRET PASSAGEWAYS, A UNESCO designation and a 260-foot tower with not one but 12 turrets, Alcazar of Segovia is a castle for the history books. In fact, it has housed the General Military Archive since 1898. "Record office" hasn't been its only function over the centuries, however: It has also served as a medieval fortress, a royal palace, a military prison and the Royal Artillery College.

Built during the 11th century on the site of a Roman fortress, the Alcazar became a royal residence in the 13th century. It took on a Gothic appearance under the reigns of kings John II and Henry IV in the 1400s. In 1474, the palace hosted the coronation of Queen Isabella I, who was instrumental in the political unification of Spain (and the sponsor of an explorer by the name of Christopher Columbus).

King Alfonso XII initiated restoration work on the castle after a fire nearly destroyed it in 1862. Today it's one of Spain's most-visited monuments—an imposing ship-shaped citadel that, from its rocky perch, guards the city of Segovia. Travelers stream through its sumptuous rooms, from the Sala de las Piñas (featuring hundreds of pineapple-shaped "stalactites" stippling the ceiling) to the Kings Chamber, with 52 gold-plated figures of influential Spanish monarchs.

Most dazzling is the view from the Tower of Juan II, where guests climb a 152-step spiral staircase to gaze over the medieval neighborhoods of Segovia. This sweeping vista—once admired by Castilian royalty—is sure to be remembered for years and years to come.

SOUTHERN EUROPE

Castillo de Coca is open for guided tours daily during midday and late-afternoon hours; check castillodecoca.com for ticket prices and specific hours (the website is in Spanish only, so use Google Translate to ascertain tour details). Located in the medieval walled town of **Coca** (formerly Cauca, the birthplace of the Roman emperor Theodosius), the castle is easily reached on a day trip from **Madrid** or **Salamanca**.

Castillo de Coca

COCA, SPAIN

Built on flat land rather than on a hill, the castle required a wide, deep moat for defense.

SOMETIMES THE RIGHT ARCHITECTURAL mix can be magical. Two of the world's most distinctive historic styles—Flamboyant Gothic and Moorish—blend to magnificent effect in this 15th-century fortress in central Spain. Looking almost like a special-effects castle created for a Hollywood blockbuster, Castillo de Coca was built by Don Alonso de Fonseca, the Archbishop of Seville, in the military Mudéjar style. One of the most impressive examples of its kind (Mudéjar fortresses were built by Islamic craftsmen living under Christian reign), it was declared a national monument in 1931.

With its imposing square silhouette and 8-foot-thick brick walls, this castle was designed to withstand enemy attack—but was also embellished with striking geometric designs within the brickwork. Its polygonal (many-sided) structure gives it dramatic dimension, as do its abundant turrets (there are almost too many to count).

The center courtyard is Renaissance in style, but within the castle proper, geometric patterns and tiles typical of Mudéjar design decorate several rooms on the guided tour. Particularly noteworthy are the red, white and blue mosaics on the vaulted ceiling of the Weapons Room (or Armory).

From the Lookout atop the Tower of Homage (the keep), visitors can enjoy views of the surrounding pine forest—and a precarious peek down 13 stories to the battlements below.

The castle sits on the site of ancient Cauca, the birthplace of Roman emperor Theodosius.

SOUTHERN EUROPE

Alhambra

GRANADA, SPAIN

THE WORD *FORTRESS* SOUNDS foreboding, but when a hilltop stronghold is designed with Moorish grandeur and set in sunny Andalusia, the result is stunning. That's the Alhambra, named for the red color of its walls (*qa'lat al-Hamra* means Red Castle in Arabic). Its origins trace back to the 13th century, when Muhammad I of the Nasrid dynasty established a royal residence here. But it was Yusuf I and Muhammad V, in the 14th century, who dreamed up the structures we most appreciate today: the Nasrid Palaces, the Patio of the Lions, the Justice Gate, the Comares Room and the Alcazaba.

Visitors feel instantly in awe of the craftsmanship of the era. The Nasrid kings covered every square inch of their palaces with carvings, ceramics and plasterwork and reveled in the symmetry of grand arches and slender pillars. Travelers linger in the mesmerizing Palace of the Lions and pose against the mossy green reflecting pool of the Court of the Myrtles.

There are exceptional gardens too—if the carvings and ceramics don't make guests swoon, the cypresses and roses certainly will.

The Alhambra's extraordinary gardens include the Walk of the Cypresses, Saint Francis' Gardens and the Garden of the Ramparts.

SOUTHERN EUROPE

The Alhambra is open daily except Christmas and New Year's Day; visit alhambradegranada.org to buy tickets in advance (highly recommended). You must enter the Nasrid Palaces only during the time indicated on your ticket. Daytime tours are most comprehensive, while evening visits require choosing between the Nasrid Palaces and the gardens. Stay at **Hotel Hospes Palacio de los Patos**, a 19th-century palace in the center of town that juxtaposes the historic and the modern.

The Serallo section's reflecting pool was a symbol of the sovereign's power.

The Court of Myrtles is so named because of the bright green myrtle bushes that surround it.

SOUTHERN EUROPE

The palace and gardens are open every day; tickets include a tour of the grounds aboard a hop-on/hop-off tram. Guided tours of the palace are about $5; visit parquesdesintra.pt/en for a schedule. The hilly gardens can also be explored via horse-drawn carriage, on horseback, via power-assisted e-bike or on foot via miles of hiking trails. In operation since 1764, **Lawrence's** is said to be the oldest hotel in the country.

112 THE WORLD'S MOST AMAZING CASTLES

Pena Palace

SINTRA, PORTUGAL

Pena Palace is the finest example of 19th-century Romanticism in Portugal.

NAMED FOR ITS LOCATION ATOP Sintra's tallest peak, Pena Palace (*pena* translates to "cliff" or "rock") charms from afar with a pair of candy-colored red and yellow towers. Adding to its intrigue, the palace often appears to float above clouds of low fog that regularly roll in from the ocean.

Long before Portugal's King Ferdinand II constructed this exuberant aerie for Queen Maria II, legend has it that an apparition of the Virgin Mary appeared to a group of medieval monks who'd made their way up the mountain. They soon set up a tiny chapel, which was expanded into a monastery in the 16th century and, in 1755, almost completely destroyed by an earthquake.

Captivated by the tale, Ferdinand II acquired the site and, in 1842, began the 15-year construction of the palace. Members of Portugal's royal family resided in the palace on and off until 1910, when it was converted into a museum.

Beyond its bright exterior, Pena Palace is perhaps best known for its mix of architectural styles, which include medieval, Renaissance, Gothic, Islamic, Moorish and Manueline, a lavish style inspired by Portugal's famed seafaring explorers. Throughout the vast palace, ornate carvings, ancient tiles, trompe l'oeil murals and massive Gothic archways illustrate Ferdinand II's fascination with artistic motifs.

As the palace was being constructed, Ferdinand II was overseeing another project: the transformation of 210 acres of boulder-strewn wilderness into a Romantic-era Garden of Eden, which lures visitors into a wonderland of winding pathways, lakes, chapels, statuary and more than 2,000 species of plants.

With its colorful façade and mountaintop address, Pena Palace is visible from any spot in its surrounding park.

SOUTHERN EUROPE

Aragonese Castle

ISCHIA, ITALY

WHEN DOES A CASTLE NOT NEED a moat? When it's located on its own rocky islet. And this isn't any ordinary example of 15th-century architecture, either. Aragonese Castle is bathed in the golden glow of Mediterranean sunlight and surrounded by terraced gardens, courtesy of its setting just off the Italian island of Ischia, which neighbors Capri.

The location is so appealing, in fact, that the islet has been occupied since the fifth century B.C., when it was a Greek settlement known as Castrum Gironis. During the Middle Ages, it went by the moniker Insula Minor (Ischia itself was Insula Major). It finally became known as Aragonese Castle during the 15th-century reign of Alfonso I of Aragon, when the castle took on an appearance worthy of a royal residence. Privately owned by the Mattera family since 1912, it has been a national landmark since 1967.

A few other historic happenings also took place here: Fernando d'Avalos, Marquis of Pescara, married Vittoria Colonna at the castle in 1509. In 1655, Ischia's patron saint, John Joseph of the Cross, is said to have cured himself of the plague in the spot where a chapel dedicated to him now stands. And from 1823 to 1860, Aragonese took a darker turn as a prison.

These days, the castle's demeanor is much brighter: It dominates Ischia's harbor and is one of the area's most photographed sights.

At one point, the island was home to almost 1,900 families.

Italy's famed poet Vittoria Colonna lived and wrote in the castle from 1501 to 1536.

Aragonese Castle is open daily from 9 a.m. until sunset; check castelloaragoneseischia.com for ticket prices and details (most of the tour is open-air, and seeing the entire castle requires walking about 1.3 miles across a bridge, over pathways and up and down steps). Guided tours and ghost tours (on Wednesday nights from June to September—the Nuns' Cemetery is particularly creepy) are available too. Enjoy a lunch break at one of the castle's two cafés: **Bar Il Terrazzo** and **The Cafeteria of the Monastery**. The castle also hosts concerts, art exhibits and the **Ischia Film Festival**.

SOUTHERN EUROPE

Miramare Castle

TRIESTE, ITALY

Maximilian chose the location after his ship sheltered in the nearby harbor during a storm.

RISING WHITE AND MAJESTIC FROM THE TIP OF A PROMONTORY in the Adriatic, Miramare looks like a fantasy, and that's exactly what it is—the fantastical dream house of Archduke Ferdinand Maximilian, younger brother of Austrian Emperor Franz Joseph. Commander-in-chief of the Austrian navy for a time, the globe-trotting Maximilian was an enthusiastic patron of architecture and the arts and designed the house in an eclectic Gothic-revival style, with influences ranging from medieval to Renaissance to Byzantine. Built between 1856 and 1860 for his bride, Charlotte of Belgium, the house was exuberantly decorated and furnished in the romantic style of borrowed exoticism—and visitors today see it much as it looked when the couple left it. Especially noteworthy are Charlotte's chambers, tapestried in blue watered silk, and Maximilian's chambers, exact replicas of his quarters on his warship, the *Novara*.

Sadly, the couple's love story ended in tragedy: Having become emperor of Mexico, Maximilian was executed by firing squad in 1867 at age 34. Charlotte went mad with grief, and a legend arose that anyone who sleeps at Miramare is cursed to die young in a foreign land.

Exploring Miramare is as much about the gardens and grounds as the building itself. Working with noted landscape architects, Maximilian took a barren, rocky promontory and turned it into a verdant 22-acre botanical garden. Today's guests can ramble through English-, Mediterranean- and Italian-style gardens and enjoy stunning views of the Gulf of Trieste.

Miramare is just 20 minutes by train from **Trieste**, a sparkling Mediterranean city of piazzas, elegant neoclassical buildings, ornate churches and one of the most beautiful synagogues in Europe. For the full experience, stay at the **Savoia Excelsior Palace**, with majestic views of the sea that echo those at Miramare. Trieste is known for its coffee and café culture; experience it at **Caffé Tommaseo**, a favorite hangout of intellectuals, including James Joyce.

The castle has more than 20 rooms, still furnished with original pieces.

SOUTHERN EUROPE

Rocca Scaligera

SIRMIONE, ITALY

> Rocca Scaligera sits on the southern shores of Lago di Garda in the peninsular resort town of **Sirmione**, a two-hour drive east of **Milan**. The castle is closed on Mondays. You can buy tickets in person only, or by booking a boat tour through a local company like **Consorzio Motoscafisti Sirmione**, which includes a stop at the castle. Sirmione is also known for its pedestrians-only center, thermal baths (don't miss **Terme di Sirmione**) and the ancient **Grottoes of Catullus**. Stay at the **Grand Hotel Terme**, a lakefront retreat and spa just outside the town center.

THE WORLD'S MOST AMAZING CASTLES

Italy's Ministry of Cultural Heritage and Activities preserves Rocca Scaligera for visitors.

VISITORS MIGHT FEEL LIKE THEY'RE blasting back in time as they cross the drawbridge to Rocca Scaligera, one of Italy's best-preserved fortresses. The Scaligeri family (which ruled Verona in the late 13th and 14th centuries) ordered its construction in 1277 to protect the village and control commerce on Lake Garda. When Rocca Scaligera was completed in 1383, the area was an important point of defense for ruling nobles, who housed military supplies and their extensive fleet in the man-made harbor.

Various ruling parties further strengthened the fortress until the 16th century, when military defense shifted to another town nearby. Nobody ever took up residence in Rocca Scaligera (though prisoners were often held in the basement); it continued to serve as a port and storage depot for the town of Sirmione until the Ministry of Cultural Heritage and Activities inherited it in the 1900s.

Today, travelers can explore the castle's courtyard, walk along its crenellated stone walls and climb 150 wooden steps to the top of one of the three towers. Those who are able to make it up are rewarded with panoramic views of Lago di Garda, the Monte Baldo mountain range in the distance, and classic wooden boats bobbing in the harbor below.

This straight-out-of-a-fairy-tale castle is a pristine glimpse into northern Italy's past—and one of the world's finest remaining examples of medieval port fortification.

Pleasure boats now dock in a harbor that once protected a medieval military fleet.

SOUTHERN EUROPE

Two-hundred-year-old prisoner graffiti marks the walls of Guaita.

The ticket office sells Guaita-only passes or combination options for Guaita, Cesta and other local attractions, such as the **St. Francis Museum** and the **National Gallery of Modern and Contemporary Art**. While in town, dine at **Ristorante Righi**, which boasts a Michelin star. Stay 12 miles away in the popular beach-resort town of **Rimini**, brimming with hotels, bars and restaurants, as well as Roman ruins and other historic sights.

Guaita Castle

CITY OF SAN MARINO, REPUBLIC OF SAN MARINO

Guaita towers over San Marino's historic town center, which has been UNESCO-listed since 2008.

EVEN FREQUENT TRAVELERS COULD BE forgiven for not knowing about San Marino, one of the world's smallest countries and oldest republics. A mere 23 square miles and surrounded on all sides by The Boot, it's the last of the Italian city-states that subdivided the region in the Middle Ages. And its great symbol is Guaita, an 11th-century defensive tower that presides over the destination from 2,500 feet.

Two other fortresses also rise from the peaks of Mount Titano: Cesta (the highest) and Montale (the smallest). Since the 13th century, San Marino's high, rocky setting and resilient fortifications have protected its residents from invasion and isolated them from urbanization, contributing to the site's current charm.

Guaita's stone ramparts afford breathtaking views of the Apennine Mountains and the sister tower of Cesta, also open to the public. Likewise, sightseers climb Cesta for the classic outlook toward Guaita (a Museum of Ancient Weapons is also located inside Cesta).

Three million visitors descend on this modest nation every year—a testament to the allure of this medieval enclave, where time has stood still.

SOUTHERN EUROPE

Kyrenia Castle

KYRENIA, CYPRUS

ON THE EAST END OF THE OLD harbor in Kyrenia is a castle so steeped in history, each step inside seemingly transports you to the life and times of another epic world conqueror. Built by the Byzantines in the seventh century to protect the city from Arab attacks, it has since been renovated many times over, subjected to several sieges, and utilized by the Venetians, Ottomans, and British conquering empires, just to name a few. Custodianship of the castle was turned over to the Kyrenia Department of Antiquities in 1950, and has been open to the public since 1960.

Entering the main gate of Kyrenia is an experience unto itself. To purchase tickets, first stop at the office that sits at the front of a ramp, which would have originally been a drawbridge over the moat (now a road). Then head up a narrow path to the base of the structure. Inside, castle rooms include a 12th-century chapel, a dungeon, a cistern and two museums (one dedicated to the soldiers who've resided here, the other to the famed shipwreck off the Kyrenia coast). Don't miss the magnum opus of a visit to Kyrenia Castle: the view from the ramparts. Walking across the top walkway, guests can take in a breathtaking view of the Kyrenia harbor and the sea beyond.

122 THE WORLD'S MOST AMAZING CASTLES

An infamous dungeon once held King Peter I's pregnant mistress, who was tortured by order of his jealous wife, Queen Eleanor.

Visit the burial coffin of famous Ottoman Admiral Sadik Pasha en route to the castle courtyard.

With two museums to explore—including the Shipwreck Museum—the nominal entrance fee is quickly justified. A café offers light snacks and drinks as you traverse the rocky terrain around the castle. Open year-round, including public holidays, there is no bad time to experience the castle.

SOUTHERN EUROPE

Palace of the Grand Master of the Knights

RHODES, GREECE

ON THE NORTHEASTERN TIP OF THE LARGEST of Greece's Dodecanese islands, the UNESCO-listed Medieval Old Town of the City of Rhodes is one of the most popular tourist destinations in Europe, due in part to the Palace of the Grand Master of the Knights. Originally a seventh-century Byzantine citadel, the palace was transformed in the 14th century when the island was conquered by the crusading Catholic military order, the Knights of Rhodes.

After the Islamic conquest of Jerusalem, the Knights moved their headquarters to Rhodes in 1310 and the palace, one of the few examples of Gothic architecture in Greece, was used as a fortress and command center. There, the Knights spent two centuries defending Rhodes against Barbary pirates and other pillagers before decamping to Sicily in the 16th century, leaving behind the Palace of the Grand Master, with its spherical towers and arched gate.

The palace has more than 150 rooms, although only a few are open to visitors today. Still, the lavish structure is filled with antiques. While parts of the palace were destroyed in 1856 by an ammunition explosion, Italian architect Vittorio Mesturino worked to restore it in the late 1930s, bringing it back to its former glory. The palace became a vacation retreat for the King of Italy, Victor Emmanuel III, and later for Benito Mussolini. But when Rhodes united with Greece in 1947, the Greek government designated it as a museum. Beneath the warm Mediterranean sun and surrounded by palm trees, the Palace of the Grand Master of the Knights is a historical spectacle to behold.

Statues in the central courtyard date back to the Hellenistic and Roman periods.

Early spring and early fall are the most crowded times to visit Rhodes, but the weather is pleasant year-round. The palace is open daily for visits, but closes earlier in the off-season, November to March. Just a five-minute walk from the palace, visitors looking for a special place to stay may want to check out the eco-friendly **Spirit of the Knights Boutique Hotel**, a 600-year-old mansion that's now a family-run property with luxury suites and a verdant garden.

The UNESCO-listed Medieval City of Rhodes, Greece, comprises the Palace of the Grand Master of the Knights, built in the 14th century and restored in 1937 during the Italian occupation.

MORE TO EXPLORE

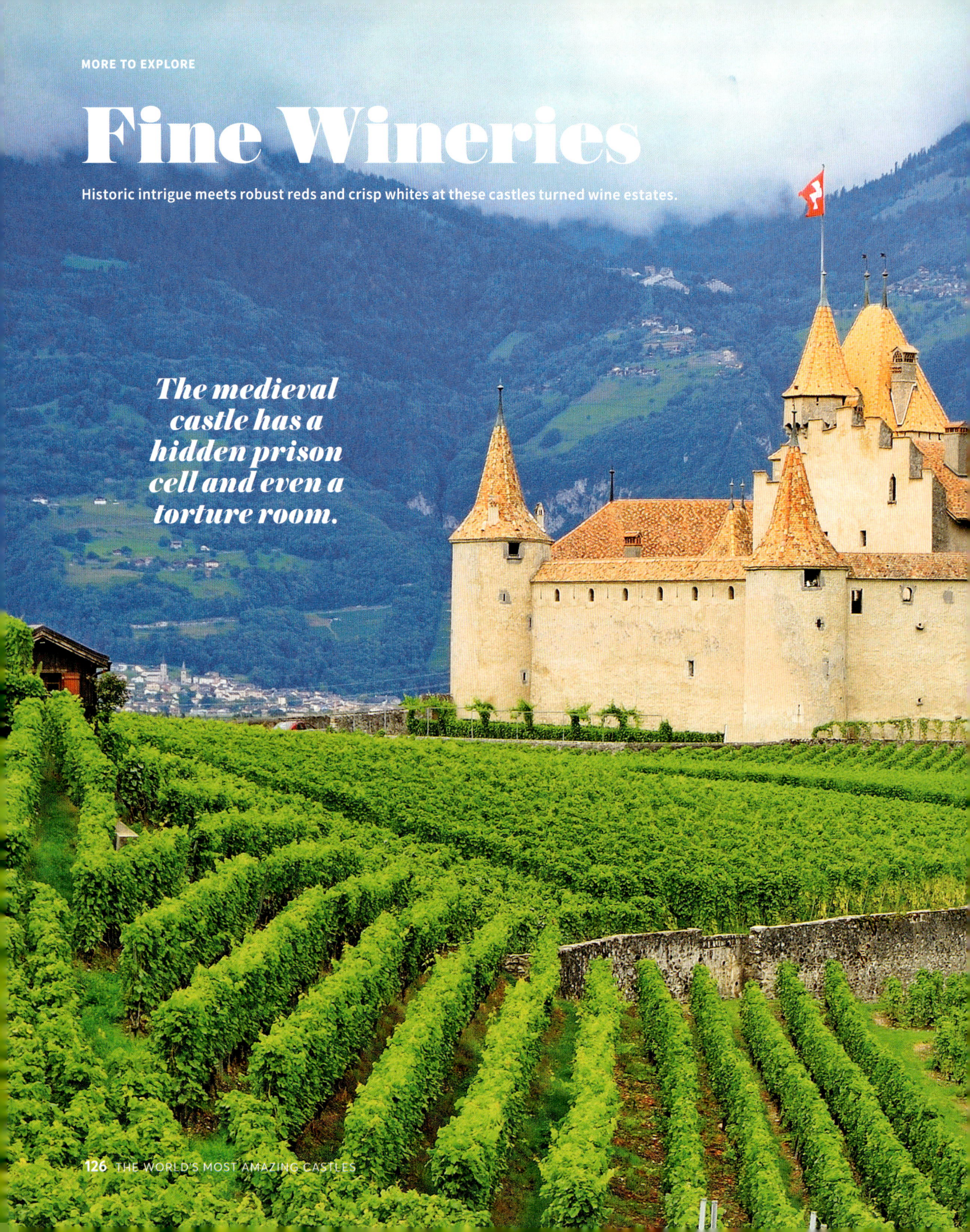

Fine Wineries

Historic intrigue meets robust reds and crisp whites at these castles turned wine estates.

The medieval castle has a hidden prison cell and even a torture room.

Aigle Castle

AIGLE, SWITZERLAND

Tucked away between the Alps and Lake Léman in the Rhone Valley just outside of Geneva, Aigle Castle's stone towers date back to the 12th century, when it played the roles of defensive stronghold, governor's mansion and prison. Now, it's the home of the Vine and Wine Museum, which offers informative and fascinating exhibits: think antique winemaking tools, corkscrews, decanters and glasses, plus modern and interactive displays that will walk you through digitally creating your very own blend of vino! However, nothing beats indulging in the real stuff, so be sit back, relax and sample some of the delicious regional wines when you're out on the restaurant terrace or in the château's cellar.

MORE TO EXPLORE

Château de Pitray

GARDEGAN-ET-TOURTIRAC, FRANCE

This 15th-century feudal manor turned 19th-century Gothic château has been owned by the same family for six centuries. Now they run four seasonal B&B suites as well as wine tastings and tours of the estate, where the same manual winemaking techniques have been used for 300 years. When you're not imbibing, explore 200 acres of forests, meadows and vineyards.

Castello di Amorosa

CALISTOGA, CALIFORNIA

Opened in 2007, this 107-room castle fulfilled the ambitious vision of winemaker Dario Sattui to create a realistic 13th-century Tuscan-castle winery, built with hand-chiseled local stone and antique European bricks. A selection of wine-tasting experiences comes with varying levels of access to the castle, including the Knight's Hall, the torture chamber, the armory and the grand barrel room.

Castello di Oliveto
CASTELFIORENTINO, ITALY

Grand dukes, popes and kings have all enjoyed fine wine and regional olive oil at this circa-1424 fortified villa—and you can, too. Wine tastings come with bruschetta, cheese and cured meats as well as a guided tour of the manor. See the wine cellar, towers, moat, courtyard and underground escape passage, and gaze at the Tuscan hillside from the top of the walls.

Castle Farms CHARLEVOIX, MICHIGAN

This French château–inspired castle was once a model dairy farm created by Sears, Roebuck and Co. president Albert Loeb. A century later, it's a wedding venue, museum, garden and tasting room serving Michigan-produced wines in the 1918 cellars, which still boast their original herringbone floor tiles and stonework.

Castello di Brolio
GAIOLE IN CHIANTI, ITALY

The Chianti region has been producing wine for two millennia, and this castle winery—the largest in the area and the oldest in Italy—boasts its own 1,000-year history. Tickets to the garden and the Ricasoli family museum include a wine tasting. Enhance your visit with a sunset tour, a vineyard picnic or an exceptional meal in the Osteria del Castello restaurant.

130 THE WORLD'S MOST AMAZING CASTLES

CHAPTER 5

Eastern
EUROPE

RUSSIAN EMPRESSES, TRANSYLVANIAN COUNTS, BOHEMIAN KINGS AND PRUSSIAN KNIGHTS HAUNT THE HALLS OF THE CASTLES DOTTING ROMANIA, POLAND, THE CZECH REPUBLIC AND BEYOND.

Visitors to Catherine Palace, in Pushkin, Russia, marvel at its colorful façade and surrounding parks.

EASTERN EUROPE

Bran Castle

BRAN, ROMANIA

THE STORY GOES THAT AN illustration of Bran Castle inspired the description of the fictional castle in Bram Stoker's 1897 novel, *Dracula*. The two castles are remarkably similar: Both overlook a river valley from a high, rocky perch in Transylvania. The main character also bears a resemblance to the real-life figure of Vlad Tepes (or Vlad Dracula, meaning "son of Dracul"), a 15th-century Romanian prince allied with the castle and notorious for impaling traitors.

Historians debate the veracity of the connection, and locals are similarly divided: Some pooh-pooh the correlation, while others capitalize on it. Like it or not, the association is here to stay.

Built in 1388, the citadel served for centuries as a fortress and a customs post before being gifted to Queen Maria of Romania by her subjects in 1920. The castle was transformed into a royal residence by the queen, whose heirs continued to live there until 1948, when they were exiled by the newly instated communist regime. It wasn't until 2009 that the castle would be legally returned to the royal family, who happily share it with an eager public.

Tourists unanimously delight in the air of mystery and foreboding that surround the castle, but the reality is far from sinister.

Bran Castle is open daily; fight fewer crowds during the October-to-March low season. Savor classic local specialties in the **Casa de Ceai** restaurant, located on the grounds. Many other attractions surround the castle, including **Rasnov Fortress**, **Peles Castle** and, farther out, the medieval towns of **Sibiu** and **Sighisoara** (birthplace of Vlad Dracula). Markets just outside the castle sell souvenirs, from Romanian handicrafts to vampire coffee mugs.

Transylvania has long been known for its belief in ghosts and legends like vampires.

Bram Stocker never visited Romania before or after he wrote the legendary Dracula *novel.*

133

EASTERN EUROPE

Malbork Castle is open daily (but closed on holidays); check zamek.malbork.pl for hours and to purchase tickets in advance. Visiting is an easy day trip from **Gdansk**. Throughout summer, nighttime tours are available, and in July, the castle hosts the **Siege of Malbork**, one of Europe's largest outdoor festivals: See Polish and foreign knight fraternities reenact military maneuvers from the 14th century.

Many rooms of the medieval castle boasted a sophisticated underfloor heating system.

THE WORLD'S MOST AMAZING CASTLES

Malbork Castle

MALBORK, POLAND

SET ALONG THE NOGAT RIVER, NOT far from the southern coast of the Baltic Sea, Malbork Castle is one of the largest brick buildings in Europe. Built in Prussia in the early 14th century by the Teutonic Knights—one of a trio of knightly orders born of the Crusades (the others being the Templars and the Order of St. John)—this onetime convent evolved over several centuries into a classic example of a medieval fortress.

Malbork Castle has quite a story to tell, having weathered tumultuous ownership changes. After being captured by Polish forces in 1457 during the Thirteen Years' War, it was neglected, then fell under the care of the Jesuit order from 1652 to 1772. That year, Malbork was recaptured by the Prussians, who stationed infantry here and deconstructed it to suit their military needs. Saved from demolition in the early 19th century, the castle began an era of extensive reconstruction—until it was occupied by Nazi Germany in 1933 and was subsequently severely damaged by World War II military operations. Postwar, Malbork was rebuilt via a public committee set up by local cultural activists.

Highlights of a visit include the Grand Refectory, the castle's largest hall, topped by an impressive fan vault; the residential Palace of the Grand Masters; and the Church of the Blessed Virgin Mary and St. Anne's Chapel beneath it, where the Grand Masters are entombed.

The castle houses various exhibits, from amber and ceramics to tombstones.

EASTERN EUROPE

Prague Castle

PRAGUE, CZECH REPUBLIC

WHILE SOME CASTLES SERVE AS historical monuments, Prague Castle still has an active role in the governance of the Czech Republic. Not only does it serve as the official residence of the president, but it's also the home of the Bohemian Crown Jewels, hidden in a vault with seven locks.

Although the crown jewels are rarely displayed, there's still plenty to see within the 111-acre complex, which comprises churches, palaces, halls, towers, terraces, gardens and fortifications. The headliner of the property is St. Vitus Cathedral, a Gothic masterpiece visible from nearly every point in Prague. Although construction began around 1340, various challenges (invasions, wars) left it unfinished until 1929.

Across the courtyard stands the Old Royal Palace, which was pressed into duty during World War II as the hiding place of the crown jewels. Art lovers can view works by Titian, Tintoretto, Rubens and others in the Picture Gallery.

Owned by a noble family, the on-site Lobkowicz Palace is filled with paintings, ceramics, manuscripts from Beethoven's Fourth and Fifth symphonies, and a version of Handel's *Messiah* that was marked up by Mozart. The Nazis confiscated the family's artwork during WWII; after the family got it back, it was taken again, this time by the Communists. After years of legal battles, the collection was again returned to the family, where it fills 22 galleries within the palace.

Prague's Old Royal Palace dates back to the 12th century.

Franz Kafka lived on Golden Lane, just north of the castle's fortified section, from 1916 to 1917.

It's free to explore the castle grounds, gardens (which are open during the summer) and the very front of St. Vitus Cathedral; touring interiors and special exhibitions requires specific tickets, as does taking photographs. For a full ticket schedule and opening hours, visit hrad.cz/en/prague-castle-for-visitors. Although the changing of the guard occurs every hour, the noon ceremony includes music and the full fanfare. Prague is rich in musical heritage; to celebrate it, each floor at the **Aria Hotel** is dedicated to a different genre.

EASTERN EUROPE

Hluboká Castle

HLUBOKÁ NAD VLTAVOU, CZECH REPUBLIC

IF HLUBOKÁ CASTLE LOOKS familiar, there's a good reason: When its owners, the Schwarzenberg family of southern Bohemia, began an ambitious reconstruction project in the mid-1800s, they chose none other than Windsor Castle as their model. Having become enamored of Tudor and Elizabethan architecture during numerous visits to England, Jan Adolf Schwarzenberg II and his wife, Eleanora, created a gem of neo-Gothic splendor, boasting 11 towers and 140 rooms resplendent with carved paneling, coffered ceilings, lead-glass windows, crystal chandeliers, valuable tapestries and ornate furnishings, almost all of which are original. Visitors today walk through rooms that look much as they did more than a century ago.

Hluboká wasn't always a private home. Originally built in the 13th century for King Premysl Otakar II, it occupied a well-defended position on a rocky hill above the Vltava River—hence the name, Hluboká nad Vltavou. A succession of private owners held it until the Schwarzenberg family took possession in 1661.

Any visit to Hluboká should include time to explore the gardens; records from 1851 show landscapers importing nearly 14,000 trees and shrubs in that one year alone.

During the 1700s, the Bohemian aristocracy was also strongly influenced by French culture, and the castle's grounds included an elaborate two-story stable building, which today houses the Ales South Bohemian Art Gallery. The only art museum in the region, it's free, and worth a visit for its collection of Dutch paintings and Gothic art.

Hluboká's gardens were recreated according to the English model.

Hluboká is noted for its weaponry collection and the expansive view from its lookout tower.

From Prague, it's possible to visit Hluboká as a day trip by train or bus; you can also book a tour that includes the castle in a visit to the historic town of **Cesky Krumlov**, a UNESCO World Heritage site with more than 300 historic buildings, including its own castle. Even better, give yourself time to explore Cesky Krumlov's Old City by staying a night or two: Good choices include the elegant boutique **Hotel Garni Villa Beatika** or the romantic **Hotel Bellevue**.

EASTERN EUROPE

Karlštejn Castle

KARLŠTEJN, CZECH REPUBLIC

AS VISITORS MAKE THE 30-MINUTE walk up a scenic hillside to Karlštejn Castle, the medieval gem comes into spectacular focus. Like giant stairs stepping up a forested slope, the site's three main buildings ascend physically, symbolically —and aesthetically.

At the base is the Burgrave's House, a residence for the king's deputy. Here, sightseers pause to observe a 260-foot-deep well, once powered by a manually operated wheel. On the next level is the five-story Imperial Palace, holding the chambers of Charles IV, King of Bohemia and Holy Roman Emperor, who built the castle from 1348 to 1365.

Capping the royal trifecta is the 200-foot-high Great Tower, which shelters the Chapel of the Holy Cross. A safe house for the Czech crown jewels and the crown jewels of the Holy Roman Empire for some 50 years, the chapel also protected the king's menagerie of holy relics. Inside hangs a series of 129 panels depicting saintly figures—to this day, the largest surviving collection of medieval paintings in Europe. Legend holds that Charles IV entered the space barefoot out of reverence. Modern guests leave their shoes on but still find themselves in awe, mesmerized by both the chapel's interior—adorned with more than 2,000 semiprecious stones—and its illustrious history that spans 670 years.

THE WORLD'S MOST AMAZING CASTLES

Drawing 250,000 tourists a year, Karlštejn Castle is the second-most-visited attraction in the Czech Republic outside of Prague.

The fortress protected the crown jewels, holy relics and royal archives until the 17th century.

Three guided tours are offered at Karlštejn Castle: Tour 1 (50 minutes) includes several interior palace rooms; Tour 2 (100 minutes) passes through the castle's chapels, including the Chapel of the Holy Cross; and Tour 3 (40 minutes) takes visitors up to the Great Tower. Go between May and October, when all tours are running. New exhibitions and a small cinema are under construction, slated for completion in 2023. Combine your visit with a stop at nearby **Křivoklát Castle**, which dates to the 12th century.

EASTERN EUROPE

142 THE WORLD'S MOST AMAZING CASTLES

Catherine Palace

PUSHKIN, RUSSIA

RUSSIA'S ANSWER TO VERSAILLES, Catherine Palace is a remarkable example of the opulence that surrounded Imperial Russia's tsars. Peter the Great commissioned the palace in 1717 for his wife, Catherine I. It remained a modest retreat in what is now Pushkin, 18 miles south of St. Petersburg, until their daughter, Empress Elizabeth, chose the palace as her summer residence in the mid 1700s. She wanted splendor—and made architect Francesco Bartolomeo Rastrelli rebuild. The result: Catherine Palace as it stands today, with its stately columns, blue-and-white-striped façade and gilded caryatids and pilasters.

Subsequent residents continued to embellish—Catherine II took the style in a neoclassical direction in the 1770s; Ippolit Monighetti added the marble grand staircase in 1860; and it became a national museum in the early 1900s. German armies destroyed the palace during WWII, but Russia's government has since worked to restore its previous grandeur.

Guided tours allow visitors access to stunning features like the Portrait Hall, the White State Dining Room and the 10,000-square-foot Great Hall. The pièce de résistance, though, is the Amber Room: Installed in 1755, it flaunts walls outfitted with nearly 1,000 pounds of rare, semiprecious amber, which Nazi armies spirited off to Germany during WWII. No one knows where the amber ended up, but the current display is a meticulous reproduction worth seeing in person.

The palace's splendor extends from the Arabesque Hall to the Hermitage.

EASTERN EUROPE

The golden-hued Amber Room was looted by the Nazis during World War II.

Most visitors arrive from St. Petersburg; it's easiest to take a taxi or book a private tour with transfers in advance. Catherine Palace is closed on Tuesdays. Visit the website (eng.tzar.ru) for tickets and seasonal hours. Arrive early in high season (May through September) to avoid lines. Guides lead tours in Russian, but English audio tours are available. The adjacent **Alexander Palace** is currently undergoing an extensive restoration; it's scheduled to reopen soon.

144 THE WORLD'S MOST AMAZING CASTLES

Visitors can admire the gilded stucco décor of the Great Hall (main), as well as the ornate dress and dining space of the gilded age (insets).

EASTERN EUROPE

The grounds of Garibaldi Castle are available for photo shoots and special events.

Garibaldi Castle is open daily for visits to its grounds and gardens; check garibaldicastle.com for directions and details. From **Moscow**, fly two hours to the Kurumoch International Airport in Samara; from there, it's a 1.5-hour drive to the property. Once the entire tourist complex is complete, visitors will be able to enjoy modern Russian cuisine in a medieval setting at the **Garibaldi Castle Restaurant**.

Garibaldi Castle

KHRYASHCHEVKA, RUSSIA

Garibaldi Castle flaunts architectural details spanning more than six centuries.

IF STORYBOOK ILLUSTRATORS NEED inspiration for the perfect castle, Garibaldi Castle—set alongside the Samara River in southwest Russia, in the small town of Khryashchevka—surely fits the bill. Perhaps that's because the concept was to incorporate the most appealing aspects of actual historic castles all over Europe. Started in the late 20th century and still under construction, Garibaldi is Gothic Revival at its core; but the complex also aims to channel the magic of the Renaissance and Victorian eras. Sure, it's all make-believe, but so are fairy tales.

Built by private owner Oleg Kuzichkin in honor of his father, Garibaldi Arcadievich Kuzichkin, this fabulous faux castle bills itself as a place of enchantment; it's characterized by Gothic arches, English-rose windows, ivy-clad turrets, spooky gargoyles and elegant spires.

While the castle lacks a medieval history of its own, it still embraces knightly lore: Sculptures of literary and historic figures (Beowolf, Lancelot, Galahad, Arthur, Guinevere and more) grace lushly landscaped gardens.

The interior rooms, when completed and opened, will feature reproductions of medieval furniture and suits of armor. Actors in period dress will provide additional historical context and add a fun interactive element. As the vision of its builder evolves into a finished fairy-tale fortress, Garibaldi Castle will be like a Renaissance-festival-meets-*Shrek* experience that can be enjoyed 365 days a year.

EASTERN EUROPE

Swallow's Nest

YALTA, CRIMEA

HOVERING 130 FEET ABOVE the Black Sea, near the resort town of Yalta, Swallow's Nest castle seems oblivious to the controversy swirling around its location: Crimea, a subtropical peninsula stretching from the south of Ukraine. Russia has occupied the region since 2014, and the U.S. State Department has declared it unsafe for American travelers. Currently, the castle welcomes mainly Russian tourists, although it remains on "most amazing castles" lists—and for good reason.

Built in 1912, the neo-Gothic structure was the holiday residence of German oil magnate Baron von Steingel. Despite its small size, the castle quickly drew attention for its fanciful façade and precarious setting extending over the edge of the Aurora Cliff.

In 1927, Swallow's Nest withstood a major earthquake that caused part of the rock face to crumble into the sea. Afterward, the castle sat neglected for decades; more recent restorations transformed the interior first into a restaurant, then into rotating exhibition spaces.

Though few Americans will see this monument in person, it remains a proud symbol of Crimea—a disputed land of indisputable beauty.

Intrepid visitors climb 800 steps to reach this celebrated landmark.

The U.S. State Department has issued a "Level 4: Do Not Travel" advisory for Crimea and is not able to provide emergency services to U.S. citizens in the region. Determined travelers can visit by way of Russia on a Russian visa; the flight from Moscow takes 2.5 hours. Work with a reputable tour operator, such as Crimea Travels, founded by a Canadian couple in 2016. Be aware that entering Crimea without crossing a Ukrainian border may prohibit you from entering Ukraine in the future.

THE WORLD'S MOST AMAZING CASTLES

Swallow's Nest balances on a modest 1,800-square-foot foundation.

EASTERN EUROPE

Trakošćan Castle

BEDNJA, CROATIA

The pretty white facade of the castle is mirrored in a man-made pond on the estate grounds.

PERCHED ON A HILL OVERLOOKING a man-made lake, Trakošćan rises out of the rolling green countryside in northern Croatia like a vision in a fairy tale. Though its original owners are unknown, the castle was built as part of the Croatian defense system in the late 13th century, and first served as a small observation fortress. By the end of the next century, it had become a part of a large collection of palaces owned by the Counts of Celje, an influential late-medieval noble dynasty from the area of present-day Slovenia.

The ivory-colored castle with red shingled roofs changed hands frequently over the centuries, undergoing many additions and renovations. By the mid-19th century, the noble Drašković family turned it into a luxe residential manor house. The surrounding verdant English-style park and lake area became a Romanticist pleasure ground. But by 1953, the family handed the castle over to the Croatian government, which launched it as a museum.

The museum now entices visitors with displays about Croatian history and the surrounding area as well as the castle itself. With its striking neo-Gothic style and surrounding landscape, Trakošćan Castle retains its romantic feel, and a visit here is like stepping back in time.

Trakošćan is about a one-hour drive north from **Zagreb**, the capital and largest city of Croatia. Buses run from **Varaždin**, the former capital, which lies about 45 minutes east of the castle. Both cities offer numerous places to sleep and dine. **Lake Trakošćan** measures about 1 mile in length and often freezes over in the winter months. The castle is open daily.

Former castle inhabitant Count George VI Drašković is considered a pioneer of photography in Croatia.

EASTERN EUROPE

The interior courtyard of the castle is used as a stage for summer concerts, as well as for open-air movie showings.

❙ Visitors can look into several kinds of tours that include the castle, such as those offered by **Nocturnal Tours Trogir & Split**, which take you down the historic towns narrow streets founded in the third century B.C. For delicious local fare, including Dalmatian prosciutto, the romantic restaurant **Konoba Trs** is a short walk from the castle. On your way, stop for a photo op before the lovely Venetian-style **Palace Cipiko**, with its graceful balconies.

Kamerlengo Castle

TROGIR, CROATIA

For defensive purposes, the castle was surrounded by a ditch filled with sand.

ON THE HISTORICAL CITY-ISLAND of Trogir, the imposing stone-walled Kamerlengo Castle sits at the western edge of the medieval town center overlooking the blue Adriatic Sea. Named a UNESCO World Heritage site, the ancient town, connected to mainland Croatia by a bridge, is the best-preserved Romanesque-Gothic complex in all of central Europe. The castle is a great place from which to view the surroundings, including the impressive 13th-century Cathedral of St. Lawrence, which looks back at the fortress from the island's eastern side.

Built as a naval base by the Venetians around 1420, when this region was still part of the Republic of Venice, Kamerlengo provided a strong defense against the Republic's enemies. Those inside the walls were able to withstand long sieges, thanks to a well that provided fresh water—and other nearly invincible structures, including St. Mark's Tower, which marks the southeast corner of the fortress. At one time, the tower's roof was outfitted with guns to repel invaders.

Once connected to the city walls, the castle interior is now empty, but in summer it serves as an open-air cinema and performance space, and is one of several locations where the annual Trogir music festival takes place. Visitors can climb to the top of the castle's battlements and circle the walls for an amazing view of the cathedrals, historic buildings and seaport.

MORE TO EXPLORE

A Royal Stay

History and spectacular settings combine at these storied hotels.

The Birds of Prey Experience will turn you into a master falconer for the day.

154 THE WORLD'S MOST AMAZING CASTLES

Warwick Castle

WARWICK, ENGLAND

Guests of this medieval fortress turned theme park can stay in glamping tents, Knight's Village lodge rooms or luxury suites in a 14th-century castle tower. Bonus: Room reservations come with priority entrance to Warwick's attractions, including a Horrible Histories maze, dungeon reenactments, landscaped gardens, palace rooms and an interactive "Princess Tower." There's also more than 64 acres of rolling landscaped gardens to explore, so don't miss the sculptured topiary peacocks that await. For military buffs, the Mighty Trebuchet there is the largest siege machine in the world. This giant catapult is an authentic recreation of one of the biggest weapons of all time.

MORE TO EXPLORE

Chateau Herálec Boutique Hotel & Spa by L'Occitane HERÁLEC, CZECH REPUBLIC

With 13th-century walls, 17th-century towers and an 18th-century English park, Chateau Herálec has castle credentials in spades. Swim under the historical stable arches; go horseback riding through the Vysocina countryside; and drive to several nearby medieval castles, including Pernstejn, Rostejn, Namest nad Oslavou and Jaromerice nad Rokytnou.

Castello di Pavone
PAVONE CANAVESE, ITALY

This medieval citadel near Turin once braved wars and invasions; now it welcomes vacationers to its 27 stately guest rooms. Conjure good luck at the Well of Mysteries, relax in the tropical gardens, and dine like Piedmontese nobility in the ornate restaurant that serves Mediterranean dishes washed down with local wine.

Ashford Castle
CONG, IRELAND

Originally founded in 1228, this now 350-acre estate in County Mayo was the private residence of the Guinness family before becoming a luxury hotel in 1939. Modern restorations have added a spa, a billiards room, a cinema, a cigar terrace, wine-tasting tunnels and Ireland's first falconry school.

Castle Hotel & Spa

TARRYTOWN, NEW YORK

Thirty miles from Manhattan's skyscrapers is a different world—one of woodlands, turreted towers and historic manors, like this 31-room hotel, originally built between 1897 and 1910 for General Howard Carroll. Book the Explore Historic Hudson Valley package, which includes tickets to Kykuit, the John D. Rockefeller Estate.

Parador Oropesa OROPESA, SPAIN

Situated above the medieval seaside town of Oropesa, this 13th-century stronghold was the first property in Spain's unique collection of state-run hotels located in castles, palaces and abbeys. Book a stay in April, during the Medieval Days festival—it's full of period markets, jousting contests, theatrical performances and parades.

CHAPTER 5

ASIA
& the Middle East

SAMURAI STRONGHOLDS, A FORBIDDEN FORTRESS, THE WORLD'S MOST FAMOUS MONUMENT TO LOVE—THEY'RE ALL IN THESE ANCIENT LOCALES, WHERE THE CASTLES OF JAPAN, CHINA, INDIA AND MORE DEFY CLASSIFICATION.

The Taj Mahal's lush greenery, red paths, blue sky and light marble create colorful contrasts in Agra, India.

ASIA & THE MIDDLE EAST

Matsumoto Castle

MATSUMOTO, JAPAN

Japan's samurai-era castles combine strength and might with beauty and graceful details.

ONE OF ONLY FIVE CASTLES IN JAPAN recognized as National Treasures, Matsumoto Castle is the oldest remaining structure of its kind in the country. Its roots date to 1504, when it was known as the Fukashi Castle, but the complex as it's seen today was built in the 1590s by the Ishikawa clan. Located in Nagano Prefecture, this *hirajiro* (flatland castle) is also known as Crow Castle because of its black exterior.

The striking former defensive stronghold consists of five stone-and-wood buildings, all with the iconic curved and tiled roofs reflective of traditional Japanese architecture. The castle's *tenshu* (main tower) still has its original, 430-year-old stone façade and inner wooden gables. Four connected smaller towers—protected by a network of gates, stone walls and a triple moat—surround it.

Japan was a feudal system for centuries—the emperor designated rule of various areas of land to different powerful daimyo (clans), shogun (warlords) and samurai families—and 23 lords ruled Matsumoto Castle until 1871, when the city took ownership.

Inside, visitors can climb the *tenshu*'s steep wooden staircases, peek through narrow windows for views of the Japanese Alps, and visit the gun museum, a collection of ancient Japanese weaponry. The castle is a popular backdrop for photo shoots, and depending on the time of year—when cherry blossoms bloom in the spring or fall foliage blankets the grounds—the scene is a storybook glimpse into the country's culture and past.

From **Tokyo**, take the Super Azusa express train from Shinjuku Station (2.5 hours). The castle is a 15-minute walk from Matsumoto Station; or book a town tour with **Town Sneaker Bus**, which stops at the castle. Matsumoto Castle is open daily; visit matsumoto-castle.jp for hours. Cherry blossoms bloom in April, and the **Taiko Drum Festival** is held in July. English-language tours are available April through October.

The red Uzumibashi Bridge pops against Matsumoto Castle's black façade.

161

ASIA & THE MIDDLE EAST

Himeji Castle

HIMEJI, JAPAN

THE FIRST THING VISITORS DISCOVER upon entering Himeji Castle, built in 1609, is how easy it is to get lost. The maze of passages connecting the three watchtowers was designed to confuse invaders, thus preventing them from reaching the central keep.

Other defensive features include a moat, 84 gates (21 are still intact) and windows with mechanisms for dropping stones on enemies below. As it happens, the castle never did come under attack, and a five-year program of extensive renovations has also contributed to its impressive state of preservation.

Both a UNESCO site and a Japan National Treasure, Himeji Castle is one of the largest castles in the country, featuring 75 buildings connected by intersecting paths. Its multiple white-plastered tiers, resembling a bird with beating wings, earned it the nickname the White Heron Castle. The surrounding wall dates from 1346, when warlord Toyotomi Hideyoshi first established a stronghold here.

Savvy sightseers keep an eye out for architectural subtleties designed to indicate status. For example, in Princess Senhime's quarters of Nishinomaru, the corridor slants gradually upward, elevating each room slightly above the next to reflect the rank of the resident.

Just inside the Hishi gate, the outer garden is free and open to the public, and its cherry tree–lined paths and green lawns are popular for walking and picnicking.

By bullet train, Himeji Castle is 30 minutes from **Osaka** and 45 minutes from **Kyoto**. In the latter, the **Hotel Granvia Kyoto** is conveniently located right next to Kyoto Station and its selection of authentic restaurants, including **Hashitate** and **Katsukura**. Bring or download a guidebook prior to visiting the castle, where signage is minimal, particularly in the interior. If you come to the castle on a Saturday, Sunday or holiday, boat rides are available on the moat.

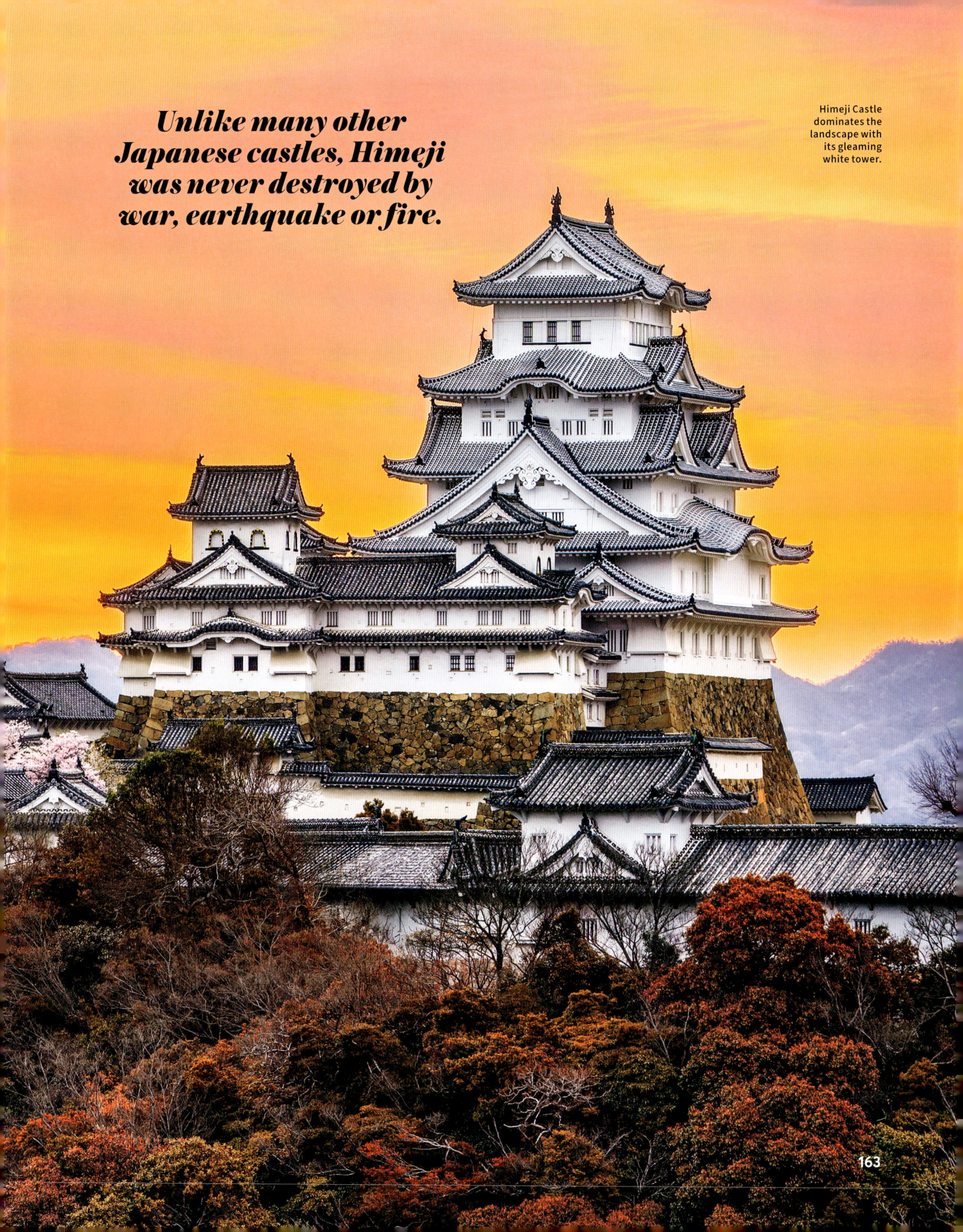

Unlike many other Japanese castles, Himeji was never destroyed by war, earthquake or fire.

Himeji Castle dominates the landscape with its gleaming white tower.

ASIA & THE MIDDLE EAST

Osaka Castle

OSAKA, JAPAN

NOW A REFUGE IN A BUSTLING commercial metropolis, Osaka Castle (Osakajo) was not always the peaceful oasis it is today. Built in 1583 by general Toyotomi Hideyoshi—sometimes described as the Napoleon Bonaparte of Japan—it was the largest castle in Japan and intended to unify the country. But by 1600, Hideyoshi was dead—and soon the Tokugawa shogunate was in control, winning the castle in 1615.

Thus began a tumultuous time in history, during which the castle was demolished and rebuilt repeatedly, often for military purposes. Restored in 1931 as a military arsenal, it was bombed during World War II and finally reconstructed in 1997.

From its expansive observation platform high on a hill, Osaka Castle offers spectacular views of the city. Inside the main tower is the castle museum, which houses eight floors of collections, including samurai costumes that are available to try on.

Enclosed by a network of walls and moats, the grounds encompass almost 500 acres of parklands and amenities, including a bandshell, a sports arena, a garden with a teahouse and more than 600 cherry trees. Popular with both locals and tourists, the castle's park hosts frequent free concerts, and street performers draw large crowds.

Ancient and modern converge in Osaka, a thriving urban center with a population of 2.6 million people.

Located in the tourist heart of the city, somewhat east of the downtown business district, Osaka Castle is served by numerous train and subway lines. The nearby **Tanimachi** neighborhood is packed with popular local restaurants; for a quick lunch, try traditional *unagi* (eel) at **Nishihara** or hit up a noodle shop such as **Menya Ageha** (ramen) or **Tokumasa Udon** (udon). **Hotel New Otani Osaka** is known for its castle views.

THE WORLD'S MOST AMAZING CASTLES

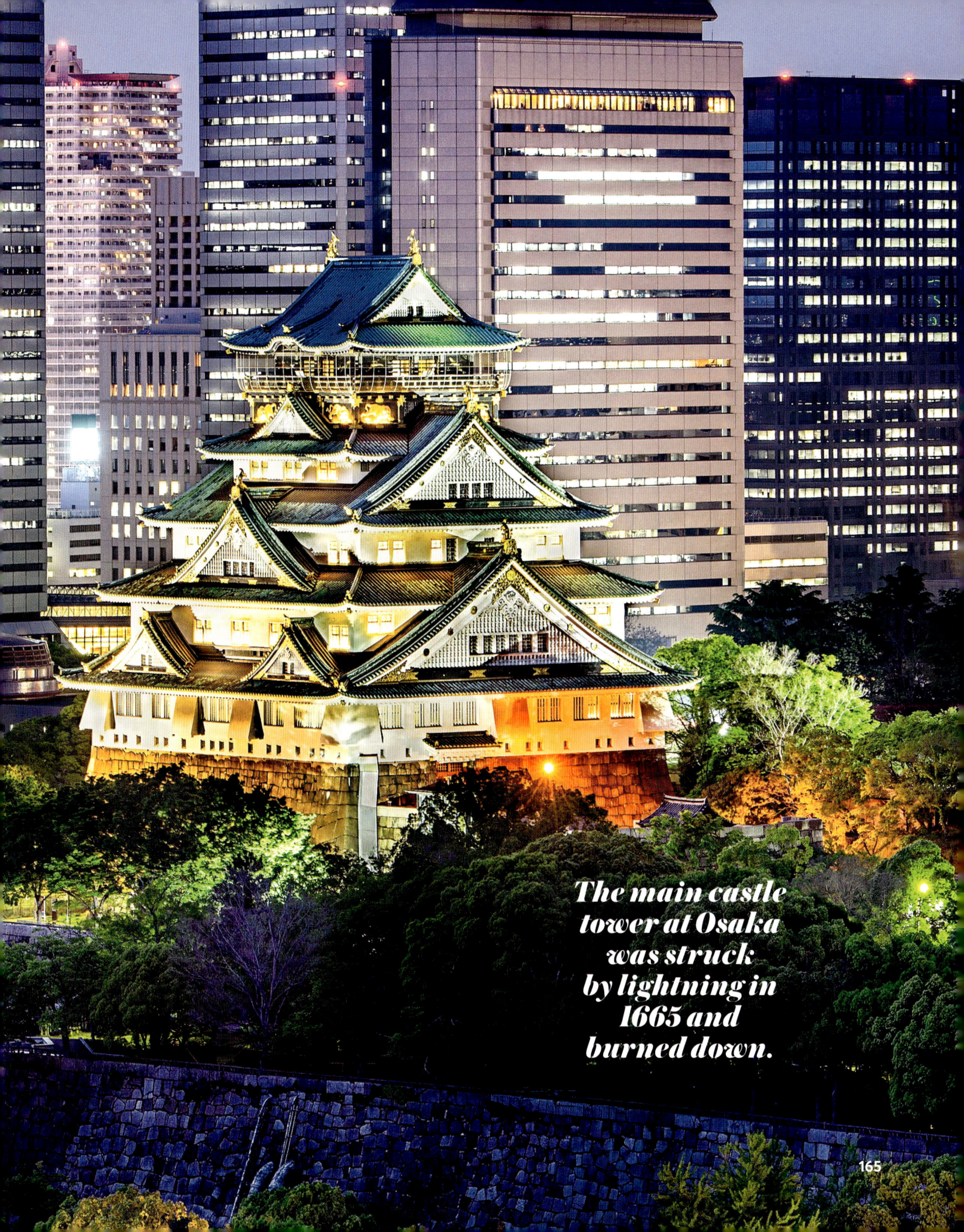

The main castle tower at Osaka was struck by lightning in 1665 and burned down.

ASIA & THE MIDDLE EAST

The Forbidden City limits visitors to 80,000 a day, which tells you how crowded it can get. If possible, go on a weekday—ideally as soon as the gates open. Leave at least three hours to see the entire 180-acre complex, then seek out the roast duck at **Siji Minfu** or **Dawan Ju**, both known for Beijing's signature dish. Continue the history theme by staying at **Beijing Double Happiness Hotel**, a 250-year-old inn located in the vibrant **Dongsi** neighborhood.

Forbidden City

BEIJING, CHINA

The Forbidden City is considered the crown jewel of Chinese artistic and architectural achievement.

AS THE LARGEST IMPERIAL PALACE IN the world, China's Forbidden City sits at the top of many travelers' wish lists. A UNESCO World Heritage site since 1987, it's China's most popular tourist attraction, with more than 14 million visitors entering its famed Meridian gate every year.

Dating from 1420, during the early Ming dynasty, the Forbidden City was the residence of every Chinese emperor—24 in all—until it was opened to the public at the start of the revolution in 1925. Because the emperor was considered a son of god, the palace was thought to be divine and therefore forbidden to commoners.

It took more than a million workers to construct the palace over a 14-year period. Highlights include the Hall of Supreme Harmony, with its massive carved marble slab depicting the march of dragons; the Emperor's throne, in the Palace of Heavenly Purity; the elegant Manchurian architecture of the Palace of Earthly Tranquility; and the world's greatest collection of jade artifacts. Every building and room is rich in detail, with intricately carved eaves, coffered ceilings, embossed tile work and colorful murals.

After exiting the north gate, Jingshan Hill is straight ahead, offering those who climb it the classic panoramic view of the Forbidden City.

Fascinating sights within China's Forbidden City include the Hall of Complete Harmony and the six pairs of bronze lions.

ASIA & THE MIDDLE EAST

Bodrum Castle

BODRUM, TURKEY

The knights put hundreds of painted coats of arms and reliefs on the walls above the gates; 249 remain today.

THE KNIGHTS OF SAINT JOHN KNEW A pretty spot when they saw one, and Bodrum Castle is the proof. Set on a rocky peninsula between two sapphire-hued bays on the southwest coast of Turkey, the 15th-century castle they constructed is named for the town where it stands—now a seaside hot spot with five-star resorts—but is also known as the Castle of St. Peter.

The original layout of this UNESCO site is still intact. Medieval Gothic in design, it features five distinct towers that represent the nations from which the knights hailed: France, Spain, Germany, Italy and England. These Crusaders also decorated the castle's towers and walls with coats of arms and carved reliefs, of which more than 200 remain—including the coat of arms of King Henry IV, on the English Tower.

The Knights ruled for 120 years, until the castle was claimed by Sultan Suleiman I in 1522. The Ottoman ruler didn't live here with his legendary harem (Topkapi Palace in Istanbul displays the spoils of the empire) but made it a small garrison; by 1895, it was a full-fledged prison. Bodrum Castle was bombed during World War I, then taken over by invading Italians.

It wasn't until the 1921 War of Independence under Mustafa Kemal (better known as Ataturk) that the fortress was back in Turkish hands. While it served as a military base during WWII, this landmark now plays a more cultural role: housing a fascinating collection of artifacts from ancient shipwrecks.

The monument and the **Museum of Underwater Archaeology** are located in the center of Bodrum, which is reachable by plane from **Istanbul** or a three-hour drive from **Izmir**. Live in the lap of luxury at **Mandarin Oriental, Bodrum**, and visit ancient sites like the **Mausoleum of Mausolus** and the **Bodrum Amphitheater**.

Bodrum Castle overlooks the port city's inviting Kumbahce Bay.

ASIA & THE MIDDLE EAST

The Amber Fort was designed using Rajput (Hindu) and Mughal (Islamic) styles.

Check out an impressive reflection of the fort in the adjacent Maota Lake.

Amber Fort, located about seven miles outside of Jaipur, is open daily from 8 a.m. to 5:30 p.m.; check tourism.rajasthan.gov.in/amber-palace.html for ticket info. The palace complex is massive, so definitely hire a guide or purchase an audio guide. There's also an evening sound-and-light show starting at 7 p.m. Redeem your Marriott Rewards points at **Le Meridien Jaipur Resort & Spa**, overlooking the Aravalli Hills.

170 THE WORLD'S MOST AMAZING CASTLES

Amber Fort

JAIPUR, INDIA

GETTING UP TO THE AMBER FORT, perched commandingly on a ridge in the Indian state of Rajasthan, can be an adventure—the traditional way to arrive is by elephant. Every morning, they're lined up at the lower entrance, waiting for tourists to be hoisted up before making their way—often amid high heat and heavy dust—up to the fort. Out of concern for the animals' welfare, this method is no longer favored, so alternately, visitors can walk 10 to 15 minutes or wait in line for a four-wheel-drive vehicle.

On arrival, stepping through the Suraj Pol (Sun Gate) and touring this UNESCO site is a visual delight. Built in the late 16th century by Raja Man Singh, this sandstone-and-marble complex of palaces and temples was the main residence of the Rajput Maharajas.

There is much to admire within the monument: the splendid silver doors of the Shila Devi Temple; the elephant-topped columns of the Diwan-i-Aam (Hall of Public Audience); the frescoed arches of the Ganesh Pol, which leads to the Maharajah's residence; the elaborate mosaics of the Jai Mandir (Hall of Victory); and the ivory-inlaid sandalwood floor of the Sukh Niwas (Hall of Pleasure).

Even before arriving, the Amber Fort (aka Amer Fort) is visible for miles, which adds to its mystique. Travelers would be wise to check their cameras' remaining storage ahead of time, if they want to capture every stunning detail.

ASIA & THE MIDDLE EAST

Sunrise is a magical time to view the monument from a distance.

The Taj Mahal's white-marble walls are inlaid with intricate patterns of precious and semiprecious stones.

172 THE WORLD'S MOST AMAZING CASTLES

Taj Mahal
AGRA, INDIA

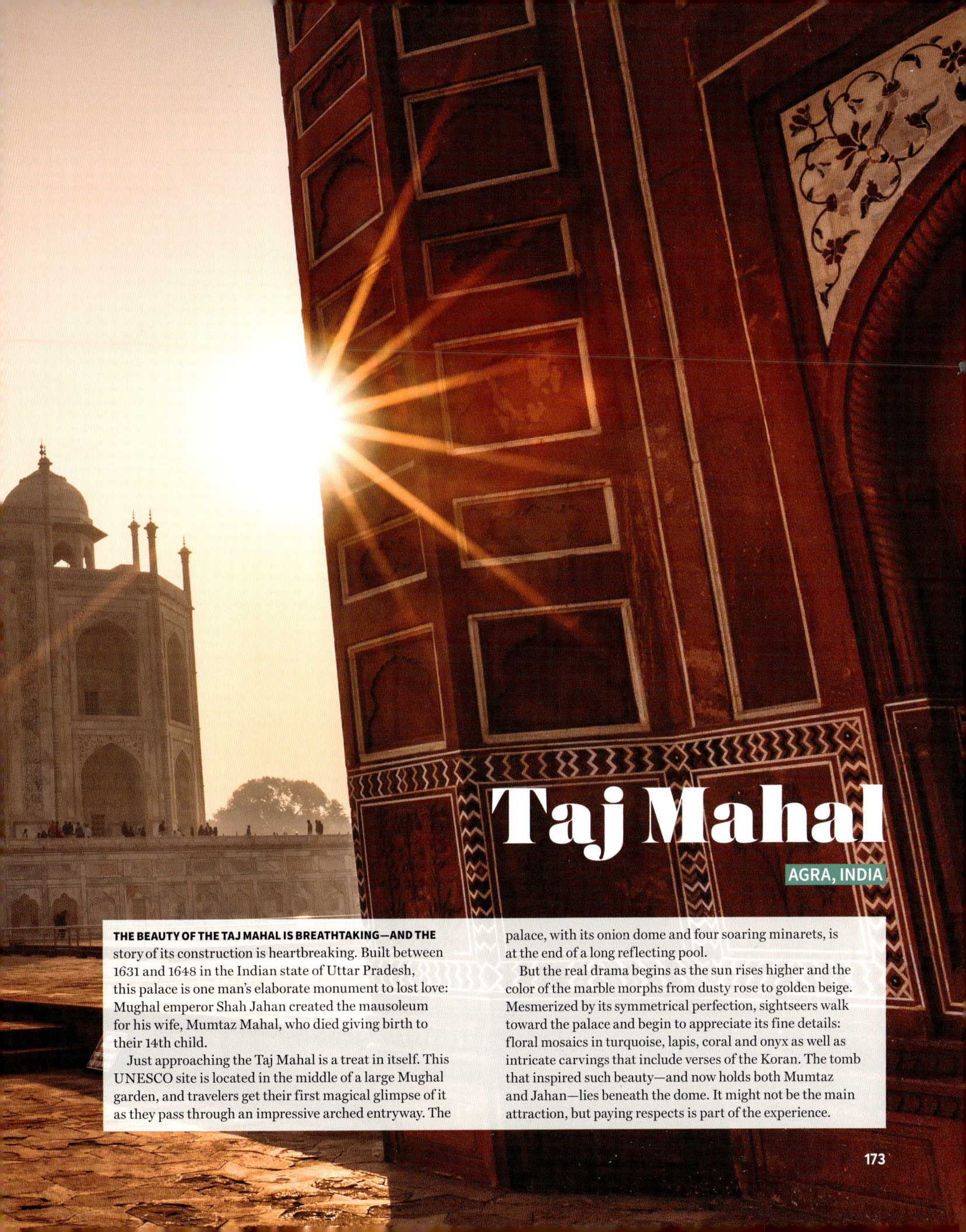

THE BEAUTY OF THE TAJ MAHAL IS BREATHTAKING—AND THE story of its construction is heartbreaking. Built between 1631 and 1648 in the Indian state of Uttar Pradesh, this palace is one man's elaborate monument to lost love: Mughal emperor Shah Jahan created the mausoleum for his wife, Mumtaz Mahal, who died giving birth to their 14th child.

Just approaching the Taj Mahal is a treat in itself. This UNESCO site is located in the middle of a large Mughal garden, and travelers get their first magical glimpse of it as they pass through an impressive arched entryway. The palace, with its onion dome and four soaring minarets, is at the end of a long reflecting pool.

But the real drama begins as the sun rises higher and the color of the marble morphs from dusty rose to golden beige. Mesmerized by its symmetrical perfection, sightseers walk toward the palace and begin to appreciate its fine details: floral mosaics in turquoise, lapis, coral and onyx as well as intricate carvings that include verses of the Koran. The tomb that inspired such beauty—and now holds both Mumtaz and Jahan—lies beneath the dome. It might not be the main attraction, but paying respects is part of the experience.

ASIA & THE MIDDLE EAST

The ornate cenotaphs are just for show: The real sarcophagi are at the garden level. Intricate archways add depth to the interior (inset).

The Taj Mahal is open Saturday through Thursday, from sunrise to sunset; check tajmahal.gov.in for directions and tickets. Located on the outskirts of Agra, about 127 miles from **Delhi**, the palace is one of India's most-visited sites, so expect crowds, especially at sunrise and sunset. Full-moon visits are also possible once a month. Also see the UNESCO sites of **Fatehpur Sikri** and the **Red Fort of Agra**, both fortified cities that date to the 16th century.

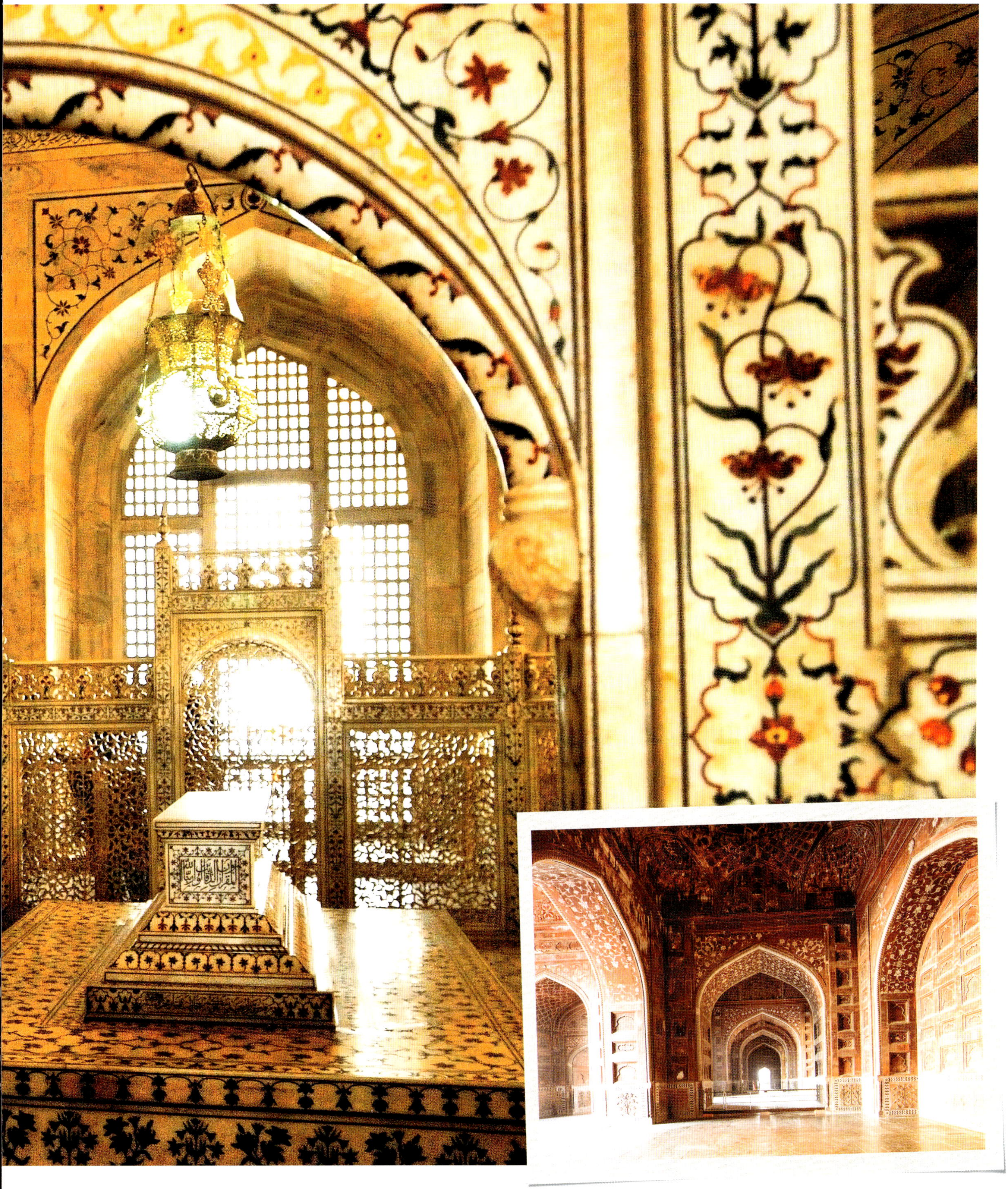

ASIA & THE MIDDLE EAST

Watchtowers, like those of Jahili Fort, are an important part of Emirates' architectural heritage.

> The Al Jahili Fort is open year-round, Tuesdays through Sundays, with limited hours on Fridays, but you may want to plan your visit around the cooler months. The best time to go is between October and April, when the weather is more comfortable, but also more humid. In summer, the average temperature can reach a dry 110 degrees Fahrenheit! The city of Al Ain offers several resort options, including the **Radisson Blu Hotel** and the **Al Ain Rotana**, where visitors can relax or enjoy a swim in the pool.

Al Jahili Fort

AL AIN, UNITED ARAB EMIRATES

Al Ain and its oases were named the first UNESCO site in the UAE in 2011.

SURROUNDED BY A LUSH, AWARD- winning park, the fort, which resembles a massive, intricate sandcastle, was built in the late 1890s by then-ruler Sheikh Zayed bin Khalifa. The Sheikh would use the fort as a stronghold from which to control the tribes of the Al Ain region—but also, he wanted a summer retreat from the blistering temperatures of the Abu Dhabi coast. Because the nearby Al Jahili Oasis was fertile with fresh water, he and his family could enjoy the less-humid climate in the hot months.

The fort sits in the southern part of the Emirates' largest inland city, Al Ain, which is about a 90-minute drive from both Dubai and Abu Dhabi. Always imposing, the original structure included the high, square walls and a round tower made up of four consecutively rising and narrowing tiers. Three more towers were eventually added, one of which served as the sheikh's reception area.

Following Zayed's death in 1909, the Fort's ownership is somewhat vague but it eventually fell into disrepair, until British forces arrived in the 1950s and claimed it for their regional headquarters. The military use of the fort continued until around 1970.

More recently, in 2007-08, Al Jahili Fort underwent major renovations and was turned into an exhibition space, including for a permanent show dedicated to writer and explorer Wilfred Thesiger, a British military officer who crossed the Empty Quarter of the Arabian peninsula by foot and camel in the 1940s. Now visitors, too, can explore this magnificent historic structure.

ASIA & THE MIDDLE EAST

Tower of David

JERUSALEM, ISRAEL

LOCATED JUST SOUTH OF THE historic Jaffa Gate, marking the entrance to the Old City of Jerusalem, the medieval fortress known as the Tower of David rises as the symbol of the city as it has done since as far back as the eighth century B.C. Built on the highest point of the southwestern hill of Jerusalem, the walls of the structure have gone through numerous changes over more than 20 centuries, but have always stood as protection for the historic city.

The citadel as we know it today was built in the mid-16th century by Ottoman sultan Suleiman the Magnificent, who ruled from 1520 to 1566 and was a great patron of the arts and architecture. But the roots of the Tower of David go back to King Herod, who improved and fortified the ancient structure at the end of the first century B.C. He added three enormous towers, one of which is the so-called Tower of David. (The name is said to be a mistake made by early Christian pilgrims who attributed Herod's tower to King David.)

Over the centuries, the citadel was used primarily for military purposes, but today it houses a museum that traces the history of Jerusalem. In the courtyard, visitors can still see remains of the ancient First Wall, while a trip to the top of the towers provides a breathtaking panoramic view of the city. Tours of the Tower of David are a unique opportunity to walk in the footsteps of history.

The Tower of David stands 144 feet tall; Herod named it Phasael in honor of his brother.

From the Tower's peak, visitors can see as far as the Judean Desert and the Dead Sea.

The Museum of the History of Jerusalem is open year-round and tickets include a visit to the towers for the stunning views, as well as a tour of the Citadel Moat and the "Kishle," a hidden underground space built in 1834 by an Egyptian ruler. The **Night Spectacular** is a sound-and-light show in which the history of Jerusalem unfolds through virtual reality images against the backdrop of the Tower walls.

ASIA & THE MIDDLE EAST

Citadel of Qaitbay

ALEXANDRIA, EGYPT

THE PHAROS LIGHTHOUSE, ONE OF the Seven Wonders of the Ancient World, once stood on the spot where the Citadel of Qaitbay now overlooks the stunning Mediterranean Sea. In fact, stones from the ruins of the original structure were used in the building of the golden 15th-century Citadel, which now rises as a shining example of Alexandria's long history as a trade center and world power.

Located on the tip of an arm of land jutting out into the sea at the mouth of Eastern Harbor, the Citadel was built in 1477 by the Sultan Al-Ashraf Qaitbay to bolster Alexandria's defense against the encroaching Ottoman Empire. Made of solid stone, the square-shaped Citadel was designed with numerous towers, walls and chambers, including a mosque featuring red-granite columns on the first of the building's three floors. When Egypt fell to the Turks in 1512, the invaders appreciated the glorious structure and used it as their own headquarters.

The Citadel eventually fell into decline until the early 1800s, when it enjoyed another golden era after being refurbished. But it was nearly destroyed during a local uprising against British hegemony in 1882 when the English bombed the area. After that, the Citadel was largely ignored until the 20th century, when the Egyptian Navy turned it into a maritime museum. The Egyptian Antiquities Organization embarked on a full-scale renovation in the 1980s, bringing the fort back to the splendor that visitors can still see today.

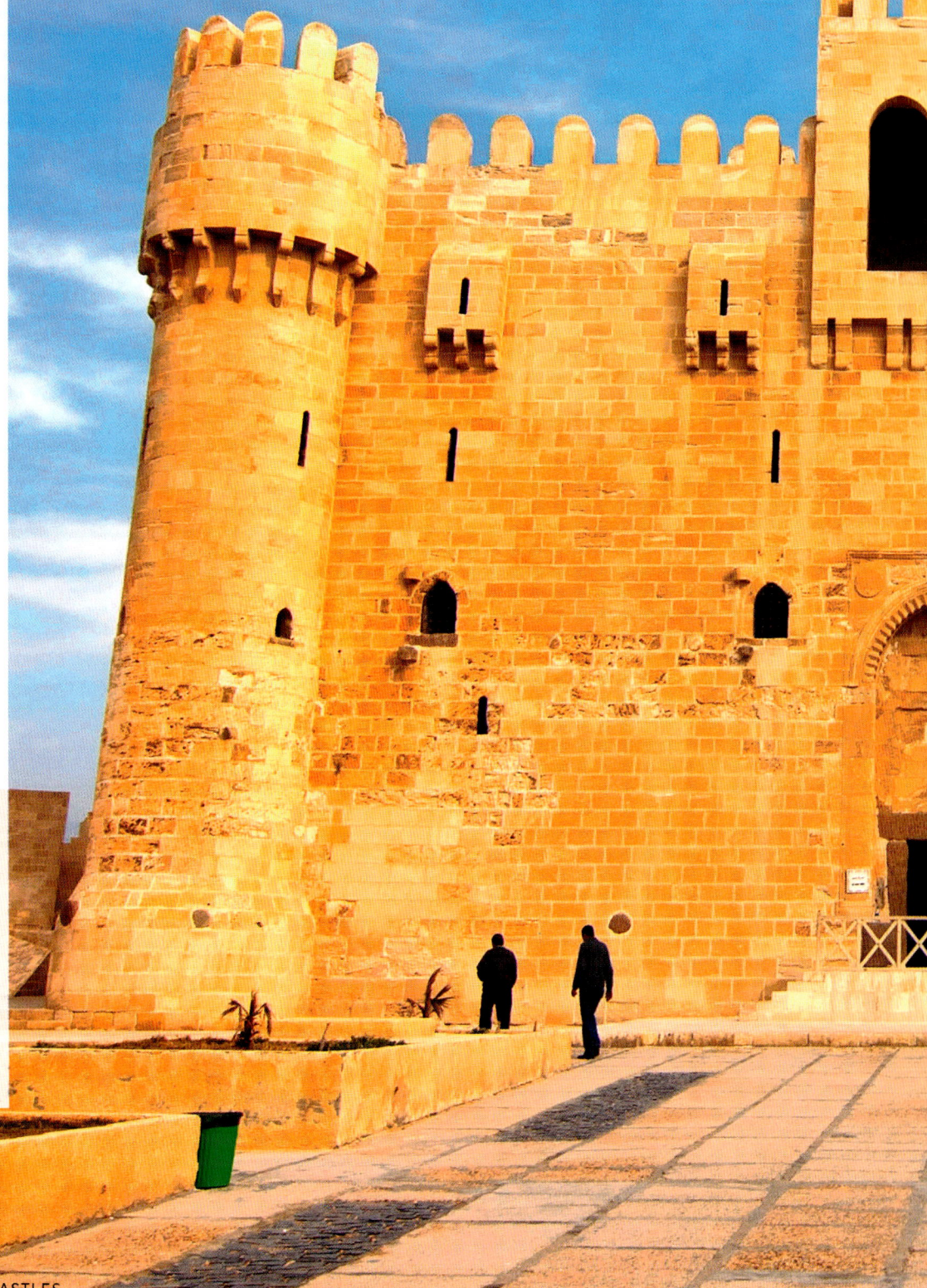

With its imposing structure and surrounded by water on three sides, the Citadel is a sight to behold!

Napoleon Bonaparte seized the Citadel, and the country, in 1798.

> The Citadel is open daily; it's best to get there early to avoid the crowds. Enjoy delicious local seafood and other delicacies overlooking the Mediterranean at nearby restaurants **SeaSide** and **Sidra by the Citadel**. Though the ancient Great Library of Alexandria was destroyed, you can visit the **Bibliotheca Alexandrina**, a creatively designed reimagining of the original that houses more than 8 million books and also functions as a cultural center and even includes a planetarium.

MORE TO EXPLORE

Awe-Inspiring Abbeys

Grandeur and reverence combine at these sublime monasteries and convents.

Visitors can attend daily Benedictine prayers from April through October.

182 THE WORLD'S MOST AMAZING CASTLES

Melk Abbey

MELK, AUSTRIA

This UNESCO site was originally built as a castle for the Babenberg dynasty, who donated it to Benedictine monks in 1089. It received a Baroque makeover in the 18th century. Tours include the monastery church, the Marble Hall, the abbey park and a panoramic terrace with sweeping views of the Wachau Valley. Be sure not to miss the centerpiece of the Abbey: its library, which houses 16,000 volumes available to the public. (More than 100,000 additional volumes are found up a spiral staircase, but those are off-limits to tourists.) Italian author Umberto Eco was so enamored with the library here that it helped to inspire his novel *The Name of the Rose*.

MORE TO EXPLORE

Mont-Saint-Michel

NORMANDY, FRANCE

Every year, more than 2.5 million people flood this evocative island monument, which celebrated its 1,000th birthday in 1966. Fortifications were added in the 14th century to protect the Benedictine abbey during the Hundred Years' War. To approach, take a horse-drawn carriage over the bay, which has the greatest tidal range in continental Europe.

Saint Catherine's Monastery

SOUTH SINAI GOVERNORATE, EGYPT

With fortified walls that date to the sixth century and a tower erected in 330 A.D., this Greek Orthodox hermitage is the world's oldest continuously occupied Christian monastery. Visit between 9 a.m. and 11:30 a.m. to pay your respects to the sacred spot where God purportedly spoke to Moses from a burning bush.

184 THE WORLD'S MOST AMAZING CASTLES

Gergeti Trinity Church
KAZBEGI, ONI, GEORGIA

With its stone bell tower and dramatic setting high in the Caucasus Mountains, this medieval monastery is one of the most-visited places in Georgia, a small Eurasian country tucked between Turkey and Russia. At certain points in Georgia's history, the remote church hid the national treasure from invaders. Take a taxi or hike the 1,400-foot climb.

Novodevichy Convent
MOSCOW, RUSSIA

This fortified cloister was founded in 1524 to sequester women from aristocratic families. Visitors marvel at the two onion-domed churches that highlight the compound: the Cathedral of Our Lady of Smolensk and the Gate Church of the Intercession. See the headstones of Russian luminaries, including President Boris Yeltsin and writer Anton Chekhov, in the cemetery.

Kylemore Abbey
CONNEMARA, IRELAND

Originally called Kylemore Castle, this circa-1868 estate on the shores of Lough Pollacappul was a labor of love from politician Mitchell Henry to his wife, Margaret. In 1920, Benedictine nuns from Belgium moved in following the destruction of their abbey during WWI. Explore 1,000 acres of woodlands, reflect in the neo-Gothic chapel and stroll the Victorian Walled Garden.

INDEX

A

Abbeys, 4, 182–185
    Gergeti Trinity Church, Georgia, 185
    Kylemore Abbey, Ireland, 185
    Melk Abbey, Austria, 182–183
    St. Catherine's Monastery, Egypt, 183
    Mont-Saint-Michel, France, 4, 184
    Novodevichy Convent, Russia, 185
Al Jahili Fort, United Arab Emirates, 178–179
Alcazar of Segovia, Spain, 104–105
Alhambra, Grenada, Spain, 108–111
Alnwick Castle, England, 42–43
Amber Fort, Jaipur, India, 170–171
Amber room, Catherine Palace, Russia, 144–145
Aragonese Castle, Ischia, Italy, 114–115
Archduke Franz Ferdinand Museum, 62–63
Argentina: Palacio de Aguas Corrientes, 101
Artstetten Castle, Austria, 62–63
Australia: Government House, 100
Austria:
    Artstetten Castle, 62–63
    Hohensalzburg Castle, 66–67
    Hohenwerfen Castle, 64–65
    Melk Abbey, 182–183

B

Bamburgh Castle, England, 44
Biltmore Estate, Asheville, North Carolina, 71
Blarney Castle, Ireland, 32–33
Bodiam Castle, Robertsbridge, England, 20–21
Bodrum Castle, Turkey, 158–159
Bran Castle, Romania, 132–133
Brazil: Ilha Fiscal, 100

C

Ca' D'Zan, Sarasota, Florida, 71
Canada: Hatley Castle, Victoria, British Columbia, 71
Carnarvon, Earl and Countess of, 10
Castillo de Coca, Spain, 106–107
Castle Howard, York, England, 45
Castles
    as abbeys. See Abbeys
    locations, 6–7 (world map). See also individually named castles or countries
    providing accommodation. See Hotels
    wineries in. See Wineries
Catherine Palace, Pushkin, Russia, 130–131, 142–145
Châteaux
    Chambord, 76–77
    Chaumont-sur-Loire, 84–85
    Chenonceau, 74–75
    Haut-Koenigsbourg, Orschwiller, 78–79
    Pierrefonds, 80–81
    Sully-sur-Loire, 72–73, 82–83
    Villandry, 86–87
    Chillon Castle, Veytaux, Switzerland, 94–95
Chile: Wulff Castle, 99
China: Forbidden City, Beijing, 156–157
Citadel of Qaitbay, Alexandria, Egypt, 180–181
Conwy Castle, Wales, 24–25
Crimea: Swallow's Nest, Yalta, 148–149
Croatia:
    Kamerlengo Castle, 152–153
    Trakoscan Castle, 150–151
Cyprus: Kyrenia Castle, 122–123
Czech Republic:
    Hluboká Castle, 138–139
    Karkštejn Castle, 140–141
    Prague Castle, 136–137
    tourist accommodations in. See under Hotels

D

Denmark:
    Egeskov Castle, 38–39
    Kronborg Castle, 36–37
Doune Castle, Scotland, 44
"Downton Abbey" (Highclere Castle), 8–11
Dromoland Castle, County Clare, Ireland, 34–35
Dunnottar Castle, Stonehaven, Scotland, 12–13, 28–29
Duwisib Castle, Southern Namib region, Namibia, 101

E

Edinburgh Castle, Scotland, 26–27
Egeskov Castle, Denmark, 38–39
Egypt:
    Citadel of Qaitbay, 180–181

St. Catherine's Monastery, 183
Eilean Donan Castle, Scotland, 45
Eltz Castle, Germany, 46–47, 58–59
England:
    Alnwick Castle, 42–43
    Bamburgh Castle, 44
    Bodiam Castle, 20–21
    Castle Howard, 45
    Highclere Castle, 22–23
    Leeds Castle, 18–19
    tourist accommodations in. See under Hotels
    Windsor Castle, 14–17
Ethiopia: Fasil Ghebbi Castle, 100

F

Fasil Ghebbi Castle, Gondar, Ethiopia, 100
Forbidden City, Beijing, China, 156–157
France:
    castles in. See Châteaux
    Mont-Saint-Michel Abbey, 4, 184
    Palace of Versailles, 88–91
    tourist accommodations in. See Hotels
    wineries in. See under Wineries

G

Garibaldi Castle, Russia, 146–147
Gergeti Trinity Church, Georgia, 185
Germany:
    Eltz Castle, 46–47, 58–59
    Heidelberg Castle, 54–55
    Hohenschwangau Castle, 51
    Hohenzollern Castle, 60–61
    Lichtenstein Castle, 52–53
    Neuschwanstein, 48–51
    Schwerin Castle, 56–57
Government House, Sydney, Australia, 100
Greece: Knights Grand Master Palace, 124–125
Gruyères Castle, Switzerland, 92–93
Guaita Castle, San Marino, 120–121

H

Hearst Castle, San Simeon, California, 68–69
Heidelberg Castle, Germany, 54–55

Herbert, George, 8th Earl of Carnarvon, 10
Herbert, Lady Fiona,
    8th Countess of Carnarvon, 8–11
Highclere Castle, Hampshire, England 22-23
    history of, 8–11
    interiors of, 10–11
Himeji Castle, Japan, 162–163
Hluboká Castle, Czech Republic, 138–139
Hohensalzburg Castle, Austria, 66–67
Hohenschwangau Castle, Germany, 51
Hohenwerfen Castle, Austria, 64–65
Hohenzollern Castle, Germany, 60–61
Hotels, 34–35, 154–157
    Ashford Castle, Ireland, 156
    Castello di Pavone, Italy, 156
    Castle Hotel and Spa, New York, 157
    Chateau Herálec Boutique Hotel & Spa by L'Occitane,
    Czech Republic, 156
    Dromoland Castle, Ireland, 34–35
    Parador Oropesa, Spain, 157
    Warwick Castle, England, 154–155

I

Ilha Fiscal, Guanbara Bay, Brazil, 100
India:
    Amber Fort, Jaipur, 170–171
    Taj Mahal, Agra, 158–159, 172–175
Iolani Palace, Honolulu, Hawaii, 70
Ireland:
    Blarney Castle, 32–33
    Dromoland Castle, 34–35
    Kilkenny Castle, 30–31
    Kylemore Abbey, 185
    tourist accommodation in. See under Hotels
    Trim Castle, 44
Israel: Tower of David, Jerusalem, 176–177
Italy:
    Aragonese Castle, Ischia, 114–115
    Miramare Castle, Trieste, 116–117
    Rocca Scaligera, Sirmione, 118–119
    tourist accommodations in; Hotels
    wineries in. See under Wineries

INDEX

J

Japan:
- Himeji Castle, 162–163
- Matsumoto Castle, 160–161
- Osaka Castle, 164–165

K

Kamerlengo Castle, Croatia, 152–153
Karkštejn Castle, Czech Republic, 140–141
Kilkenny Castle, Ireland, 30–31
Knights Grand Master Palace, Greece, 124–125
Kronborg Castle, Denmark, 36–37
Kylemore Abbey, Ireland, 185
Kyrenia Castle, Cyprus, 122–123

L

Larnach Castle, New Zealand, 71
Leeds Castle, Maidstone, England, 18–19
Lichtenstein Castle, Germany, 52–53

M

Malbork Castle, Poland, 134–135
Matsumoto Castle, Japan, 160–161
Melk Abbey, Austria, 182–183
Miramare Castle, Italy, 116–117
Monastery of St. Catherine, Egypt, 183
Mont Saint Michel, France, 4, 184
Movie sets, castles as, 42–45
Music room, Highclere Caste, England, 10

N

Namibia: Duwisib Castle, 101
Neuschwanstein Castle, Germany, 48–51
New Zealand: Larnach Castle, Dunedin, 71
Novodevichy Convent, Russia, 185

O

Oberhofen Castle, Switzerland, 96–97
Örebro Castle, Sweden, 40–41
Osaka Castle, Japan, 164–165

P

Palaces
- Catherine Palace, Russia, 130–131, 142–145
- Iolani Palace, Hawaii, 70
- Knights Grand Master Palace, Greece, 124–125
- Pena Palace, Portugal, 102–103, 112–113
- Versailles, France, 88–91
- Parador Oropesa, Spain, 157
- Pena Palace, Portugal, 102–103, 112–113

Palacio de Aguas Corrientes, Buenos Aires, Argentina, 101
Poland: Malbork Castle, 134–135
Portugal: Pena Palace, Sintra, 102–103, 112–113
Prague Castle, Czech Republic, 136–137

R

Rocca Scaligera, Sirmione, Italy, 118–119
Romania: Bran Castle, 132–133
Russia:
- Catherine Palace, Pushkin, 130–131, 142–145
- Garibaldi Castle, Khryashchevka, 146–147
- Novodevichy Convent, Moscow, 185

S

San Marino, Republic of: Guaita Castle, 120–121
Schwerin Castle, Germany, 56–57
Scotland:
- Doune Castle, 44
- Dunnottar Castle, Stonehaven, 12–13, 28–29
- Edinburgh Castle, 26–27
- Eilean Donan Castle, Kyle of Lochalsh, 45
- tourist accommodations in. See under Hotels

Smoking room, Highclere Caste, England, 11
Spain:
- Alcazar of Segovia, 104–105
- Alhambra, Grenada, 108–111
- Castillo de Coca, 106–107

St. Catherine, Monastery of, Egypt, 184
Swallow's Nest, Yalta, Crimea, 148–149
Sweden: Örebro Castle, 40–41
Switzerland:

Chillon castle, Veytaux, 94–95

Gruyères Castle, Fribourg, 92–93

Oberhofen Castle, 96–97

T

Taj Mahal, Agra, India, 158–159, 172–175

Tourist accommodations. See Hotels

Tower of David, Jerusalem, Israel, 176–177

Trakošćan Castle, Bednja, Croatia, 150–151

Trim Castle, Ireland, 44

Turkey: Bodrum Castle, 158–159

U

United Arab Emirates (UAE):

    Al Jahili Fort, Al Ain, 178–179

United States:

    Biltmore Estate, Asheville, North Carolina, 71

    Hearst Castle, San Simeon, California, 68–69

    Iolani Palace, Honolulu, Hawaii, 70

    tourist accommodations in. See under Hotels

    wineries in. See under Wineries

V

Versailles, Palace of, France, 88–91

W

Wales: Conwy Castle, 24–25

Warwick Castle, England, 154–155

Waterloo room, Windsor Castle, England, 16–17

Windsor Castle, England, 14–17

Wineries, 126–129

    Aigle Castle, Switzerland, 126–127

    Castello di Amorosa, California, 128

    Castello di Brolio, Italy, 129

    Castello di Oliveto, Italy, 129

    Castle Farms, Michigan, 129

    Château de Pitray, France, 128

Wulff Castle, Viña del Mar, Chile, 99

CREDITS

COVER RudyBalasko/iStockphoto **FRONT FLAP** Manjik photography/Alamy Stock Photo **1** graphixel/Getty Images **2-3** Jim Sullivan **4-5** (Clockwise from left) Jan Wlodarczyk/Alamy Stock Photo; RichartPhotos/Shutterstock; Phil Cooke/Alamy Stock Photo; Andrzej Olchawa/andrzejolchawa/Getty Images; Julian Elliott Photography/Getty Images; Zoonar GmbH/Alamy Stock Photo; Helmuth Rieger/Alamy Stock Photo; ¬© RAZVAN CIUCA/Getty Images **6-7** Diane Labombarbe/Getty Images **8-9** RichartPhotos/Shutterstock **10** (From top) Matthew Lloyd/Getty Images; Courtesy of Highclere Castle **11** Ilpo Musto/Shutterstock **12-13** Phil Cooke/Alamy Stock Photo **14-15** Charlie Harding/Getty Images **16-17** (From left) Jon Bower UK/Alamy Stock Photo; SuperStock/Alamy Stock Photo **18-19** Brian Jannsen/Alamy Stock Photo **20-21** aerial-photos.com/Alamy Stock Photo **22-23** NIKLAS HALLE'N/Getty Images **24-25** Ian Dagnall/Alamy Stock Photo **26-27** Sunnybeach/Getty Images **28-29** robertharding/Alamy Stock Photo **30-31** yykkaa/iStockphoto **32-33** Ian Dagnall/Alamy Stock Photo **34-35** Courtesy of Dromoland Castle **36-37** Stig Alenas/Alamy Stock Photo **38-39** giuseppe masci/Alamy Stock Photo **40-41** dleiva/Alamy Stock Photo **42-43** Keith Griffiths/Alamy Stock Photo **44** (Clockwise from top left) Prisma by Dukas Presseagentur GmbH/Alamy Stock Photo; imageBROKER/Alamy Stock Photo; Design Pics Inc/Alamy Stock Photo **45** (From top) robertharding/Alamy Stock Photo; Lankowsky/Alamy Stock Photo **46-47** Andrzej Olchawa/andrzejolchawa/Getty Images **48-49** imageBROKER/Alamy Stock Photo **50-51** (From left) Historic Collection/Alamy Stock Photo; Yury Dmitrienko/Alamy Stock Photo; Norman Barrett/Alamy Stock Photo **52-53** Daniel Smolcic/Alamy Stock Photo **54-55** Westend61 GmbH/Alamy Stock Photo **56-57** Anibal Trejo/Shutterstock **58-59** ullstein bild/Getty Images **60-61** Jon Arnold Images Ltd/Alamy Stock Photo **62-63** Borisb17/Shutterstock **64-65** Westend61 GmbH/Alamy Stock Photo **66-67** DaveLongMedia/Getty Images **68-69** John Cornelius/Alamy Stock Photo **70** (From top) Felix Lipov/Alamy Stock Photo; Ellen Isaacs/Alamy Stock Photo **71** (From top) David R. Frazier Photolibrary, Inc./Alamy Stock Photo; Kevin Giannini/Alamy Stock Photo; John Elk III/Lonely Planet Images/Getty Images **72-73** Julian Elliott Photography/Getty Images **74-75** Brian Jannsen/Alamy Stock Photo **76-77** Konstantin Kalishko/Alamy Stock Photo **78-79** Frank Bienewald/Getty Images **80-81** Hemis/Alamy Stock Photo **82-83** pedrosala/iStockphoto **84-85** Tim Moore/Alamy Stock Photo **86-87** Manjik photography/Alamy Stock Photo **88-89** (From left) Valentin Valkov/Alamy Stock Photo; Yuri Turkov/Alamy Stock Photo **90-91** Martin Ruegner/Getty Images **92-93** Lenush/Shutterstock **94-95** Alpineguide/Alamy Stock Photo **96-97** Prisma by Dukas Presseagentur GmbH/Alamy Stock Photo **98-99** Diego Grandi/Alamy Stock Photo **100** (From top) frank'n'focus/Alamy Stock Photo; frederic REGLAIN/Alamy Stock Photo; Christian Offenberg/Alamy Stock Photo **101** (From top) Stefano Politi Markovina/Alamy Stock Photo; Artie Photography (Artie Ng)/Getty Images **102-103** Zoonar GmbH/Alamy Stock Photo **104-105** JLImages/Alamy Stock Photo **106-107** Design Pics Inc/Alamy Stock Photo **108-109** Michael Cook - Altai World Photo/Getty Images **110-111** (From left) JoseIgnacioSoto/Getty Images; HAGENS WORLD PHOTOGRAPHY/Getty Images **112-113** (From top) AWP/Alamy Stock Photo; Alfredo Garcia Saz/Alamy Stock Photo **114-115** Arco Images GmbH/Alamy Stock Photo **116-117** RossHelen/Shutterstock **118-119** Henk Meijer/Alamy Stock Photo **120-121** travelbild.com/Alamy Stock Photo **122-123** ilker erdem sonmez/Alamy Stock Photo **124-125** Constantinos Iliopoulos/Alamy Stock Photo **126-127** imageBROKER/Alamy Stock Photo **128** (From top) Hemis/Alamy Stock Photo; Brian Jannsen/Alamy Stock Photo **129** (From top) Stephen Saks Photography/Alamy Stock Photo; Neyya/iStockphoto; Atlantide Phototravel/Getty Images **130-131** Helmuth Rieger/Alamy Stock Photo **132-133** Pixelchrome Inc/Getty Images **134-135** ewg3D/iStockphoto **136-137** Hans-Peter Merten/Getty Images **138-139** Hailshadow/Getty Images **140-141** Valery Egorov/Alamy Stock Photo **142-143** Yongyuan Dai/Getty Images **144-145** (Clockwise from top) Norman Barrett/Alamy Stock Photo; sinspics/Alamy Stock Photo; Norman Barrett/Alamy Stock Photo **146-147** NatalyaBond/Shutterstock **148-149** scaliger/iStockphoto **150-151** Zoonar GmbH/Alamy Stock Photo **152-153** Liubomir Paut-Fluerasu/Alamy Stock Photo **154-155** Lovattpics/Getty Images **156** (From top) Karolina Kasperova; MARKA/Alamy Stock Photo; Patryk Kosmider/Alamy Stock Photo **157** (From top) Courtesy of Castle Hotel & Spa, New York; Fotografiaismael for Parador de Oropesa **158-159** ¬© RAZVAN CIUCA/Getty Images **160-161** Prasit Rodphan/Alamy Stock Photo **162-163** Sean Pavone/Alamy Stock Photo **164-165** Sean Pavone/Alamy Stock Photo **166-167** Sino Images/Getty Images **168-169** Craig Pershouse/Getty Images **170-171** adamkaz/Getty Images **172-173** Alex Baxter/Getty Images **174-175** (From left) Image Professionals GmbH/Alamy Stock Photo; ferrantraite/Getty Images **176-177** Richard Sharrocks/Getty Images **178-179** Atlantide Phototravel/Getty Images **180-181** robertharding/Alamy Stock Photo **182-183** Rolf Hicker Photography/Alamy Stock Photo **184** (From top) Guillaume CHANSON/Getty Images; stefano baldini/Alamy Stock Photo **185** (From top) Prisma by Dukas Presseagentur GmbH/Alamy Stock Photo; kovalchuk/iStockphoto; Jose Perez/Alamy Stock Photo **BACK FLAP** Konstantin Kalishko/Alamy Stock Photo **BACK COVER** (Clockwise from top left) John Cornelius/Alamy Stock Photo; NIKLAS HALLE'N/Getty Images; Pixelchrome Inc/Getty Images; scaliger/iStockphoto; Sean Pavone/Alamy Stock Photo; frank'n'focus/Alamy Stock Photo; ¬© RAZVAN CIUCA/Getty Images; Christian Offenberg/Alamy Stock Photo; Artie Photography (Artie Ng)/Getty Images; AWP/Alamy Stock Photo

SPECIAL THANKS TO CONTRIBUTING WRITERS
Amy Cassell, Melanie Haiken, Donna Heiderstadt,
Katie McElveen, Audrey St. Clair

CENTENNIAL BOOKS

An Imprint of
Centennial Media, LLC
1111 Brickell Avenue, 10th Floor
Miami, FL 33131, U.S.A.

CENTENNIAL BOOKS is a trademark of Centennial Media, LLC

All rights reserved. No part of this publication may be reproduced, stored in a retrieval system, or transmitted in any form or by any means (including electronic, mechanical, photocopying, recording, or otherwise) without prior written permission from the publisher.

ISBN 978-1-955703-20-8

Distributed by
Simon & Schuster, Inc.
1230 Avenue of the Americas
New York, NY 10020, U.S.A.

For information about custom editions, special sales and premium and corporate purchases, please contact Centennial Media at contact@centennialmedia.com.

Manufactured in Singapore

© 2020 by Centennial Media, LLC

10 9 8 7 6 5 4 3 2 1

Publishers & Co-Founders Ben Harris, Sebastian Raatz
Editorial Director Annabel Vered
Creative Director Jessica Power
Executive Editor Janet Giovanelli
Design Director Martin Elfers
Features Editor Alyssa Shaffer
Deputy Editors Ron Kelly, Amy Miller Kravetz, Anne Marie O'Connor
Managing Editor Lisa Chambers
Senior Art Directors Lan Yin Bachelis, Pino Impastato
Art Directors Andrea Lukeman, Alberto Diaz, Jaclyn Loney, Natali Suasnavas, Joseph Ulatowski
Copy/Production Patty Carroll, Angela Taormina
Senior Photo Editor Jenny Veiga
Photo Editor Kim Kuhn
Production Manager Paul Rodina
Production Assistants Tiana Schippa, Alyssa Swiderski
Editorial Assistants Michael Foster, Alexis Rotnicki
Sales & Marketing Jeremy Nurnberg